A PHILOSOPHY OF GOD

The Elements of Thomist Natural Theology

A PHILOSOPHY OF GOD

The Elements of Thomist Natural Theology

THOMAS GORNALL, S.J.

Lecturer in Philosophy at Heythrop College

SHEED AND WARD

NEW YORK

Library of Congress Catalog Card Number 63-17140

De Licentia Superiorum Ordinis. Nihil Obstat: Robertus H. Nicholson, Censor Deputatus; Imprimatur; Franciscus, Archiepiscopus Birmingamiensis: Datum Birmingamiae, 2a Februari 1962.

Manufactured in the United States of America

CONTENTS

PART THREE—THE EXISTENCE OF GOD

FOREWORD

IN writing this essay I have had in mind chiefly Catholic readers from late secondary school years onwards including (centrally) seminarians and other such students, but I have tried not to lose sight of the needs of others who may be interested in the philosophy of God. There are a good many references to revelation even in the more strictly philosophical sections, but of such a kind that the reader to whom these seem an intrusion should be able to disengage them easily enough.

It is sometimes said that the traditional intellectual natural theology has had its day and now cuts no ice. The Thomist cannot see the matter simply like that. He holds that historically and from the nature of the case some kind of intellectual structure is necessary if religion is to keep healthy, but that religion is not merely an intellectual structure. A skeleton cannot walk, but you cannot walk without a skeleton. What would seem to be necessary in different centuries and decades is rather difference of emphasis, perspective and presentation. But these are very much needed. Whatever may be thought of intellectual approaches to God, there does seem to be room for informative writing on the subject in this country. Misunderstandings of basic Thomist concepts—that of 'necessary being', for example—are surprisingly frequent and persistent; and more than one neutral reviewer has recently expressed concern at the way writers on natural theology completely ignore relevant Thomist positions.

To what extent the present essay rightly assesses and meets a need, others must judge. That it has some unusual features of order and presentation the writer is well aware. But if it succeeds in conveying to some readers a little of what, in the history of Christianity has meant, and still means, so much to so many, it will not have wholly failed.

T.G.

PART ONE

INTRODUCTORY

I

Historical Background of Thomist Natural Theology

THE English Catholic child usually learns from the Catechism that

> *God is the supreme Spirit who alone exists of Himself and is*
> *infinite in all perfections;*[1]
> *God has no body; He is a spirit;*
> *God is everywhere;*
> *God knows and sees all things, even our most secret thoughts;*
> *God had no beginning; He always was, He is, and He always*
> *will be;*
> *God made me;*
> *God made heaven and earth and all things out of nothing by His*
> *word.*

To these basic truths about God, the Catholic is able to add the revelation of God by Himself in the Old and New Testaments and through His Church. For him the Bible is the word of God and the Church is preserved from error in her interpretation of it and in her teaching about Him.

---

[1] A more recent Catechism in use on the Continent is more intelligible to the young, and perhaps not less philosophical: *God is our Father in heaven.*

From revelation he learns that God is three Persons, and all about the incarnation of the second Person and the redemption of the world. The words and actions of Christ are the words and actions of God, because Christ is God.[1]

For the Catholic the Cross of Christ is the centre of human existence, even intellectually.

These truths about God, partly available to natural reason, partly dependent on revelation, are amply sufficient to see the ordinary busy Christian safely through life. They are much deeper to him than the non-Christian might suppose, because they are not merely learned but lived in the context of the life of the Church which touches the Catholic's life and thought at every point, or rather, which is his one true life. The Catholic, too, in a special way as a member of the Church, has available the grace of the Holy Spirit which makes it all real and domestic: 'He will teach you all things and bring all things to your mind, whatsoever I shall have said to you.'[2]

This little book is about the philosophy of God, and that raises a number of questions. What is philosophy? Is it necessary? What connection if any has it with revelation? How much can be known about God by natural reason, and with what kind of certainty?—and a number of others.

To make a start, philosophy means using our minds about the most basic things: the nature, origin and destiny of man; the existence and nature of the material and the

---

[1] It may be necessary to explain, for those unacquainted with Christian doctrine, that the doctrine of the divinity of Christ does not involve saying that divinity is, or becomes, humanity. Christ as God is a divine Person, the second Person of the Blessed Trinity. This Person took in addition human nature, so as to be one Person with two natures. The Athanasian Creed expresses this truth by saying, *Nam sicut anima rationalis et caro unus est homo, ita Deus et homo unus est Christus*—just as rational soul and flesh are the unity which is man, so God and man are the unity which is Christ.

[2] John xiv, 26.

immaterial; the existence and nature of God. Philosophy as such uses the light of natural reason alone, and borrows nothing from revelation. In theory, any man who uses his mind about these questions might, without the help of revelation, come to many of the conclusions which the Catholic holds. And, in fact, in the pagan world of Greece and Rome a number of philosophers did so. The philosophy of St Thomas Aquinas, Thomism, the official philosophy, it may be called, of the Catholic Church, has its roots deep in the philosophy of ancient Greece. One line of development in Greek philosophy finds its culmination through Plato and Aristotle in Plotinus, and passed through St Augustine to the new synthesis left by St Thomas in the thirteenth century. It is a line of development which may reasonably be seen as a unity as organic almost as the growth of a tree. After a period of neglect and misunderstanding, the philosophy of St Thomas was revived in the nineteenth century, and though still too little known in this country is vigorous and influential in the world at the present day.

I propose to begin by devoting a few pages to a brief sketch of the main schools of Greek philosophy, seeing them as samples of the way different types of mind worked and still work in the Western world on questions concerning the interpretation of the universe and the existence and nature of God.

The ancient Greeks began philosophy as we understand it about the year 600 B.C. By about 370 B.C. Plato had reached conclusions which have had, and still have, a profound influence in the Western world and beyond it. For Plato the ultimate causes of the world are chiefly two: (i) a separate world of eternal, immaterial Ideas, Forms or Patterns; and (ii) a Being he calls the Demiurge ($\delta\eta\mu\iota$-$o\upsilon\rho\gamma\acute{o}s$), the Fashioner of the world. It is not Plato's way to dogmatize about the details of more difficult points, nor always to be very clear in describing them, but he does seem to present these two ultimate realities as separate and distinct. If we combine them into one, as Plato apparently did not, we get a being not very unlike the God of Christianity. This may seem to be an arbitrary step to take, but it is less so than it seems. Plato's world of immaterial, unchanging Forms or Ideas contains the archetypes or patterns of this world; the Demiurge, the Fashioner of the world, uses the Forms as his models. Plotinus (*fl.* A.D. 250), a professed follower of Plato, envisaged the Platonic world of Forms as, roughly speaking, the mind of God, more accurately as what is contained in Mind, the first emanation of the ultimate Being which he calls the One. St Augustine on similar lines simply transferred the Platonic world of Forms to the divine mind, and St Thomas followed him in this, and has a good deal to say about the divine ideas.

Plato's world of Forms is a hierarchy culminating in the *Form of the Good* which, as he describes it, has so many points of resemblance to God as Christians understand Him that some scholars have sought to show that for Plato the Form of the Good is simply God. So far as Plato's actual words go, this would be a mistake. Plato never says the Form of the Good is God. The highest being to which he gives the name God is the Demiurge. However, the name is of secondary importance. What is more important is that he assigns to the Forms, and especially to the Form of the Good, part of the function of God as Christians understand Him, namely, that of ultimate intelligibility, and the source of the intelligibility of everything in the world. The Forms are ultimate and immaterial: so is God. They are unchanging: so is God. Plato, it seems, could not understand how anything could be both unchanging and living. Aristotle, his pupil, did not feel that difficulty to be insuperable. In one place (*Republic* 509) Plato describes the Form of the Good as being 'beyond essence'. This saying was seized upon by Plotinus and became central in his system; he saw it, perhaps correctly, as containing in germ the idea of the transcendence of God, that is, the fact that all else is incommensurable with God; in a word, God's infinity.

Plato's Form of the Good seems to be the same as what he describes in the *Phaedrus* as 'real and essential Being', and in the *Symposium*, with great eloquence, as 'the Beautiful itself'; while in the *Republic* it is said to be also 'the source of truth in things known'; and finally Aristotle states that Plato also called the Good 'One'. Thus in Plato's Form of the Good would be found those ultimate notes of all reality which later came to be called the 'transcendentals' because they are found in all categories of being, and pre-eminently in God: *being, unity, goodness, beauty,* and for Plato the source, at any rate, of *truth.*

The Platonic Forms are intelligible but not intelligent; yet Plato held that the world was fashioned by God and ruled by divine providence. Hence a living, personal Fashioner of the world had to be provided. This Being is what he calls the Demiurge—somewhat of a story-book figure, as Plato himself seems to allow. Yet even if we regard him as, for Plato, a big metaphor, as 'mythical' in the technical sense, still we cannot dismiss him as unnecessary, because Plato rightly felt him or his equivalent to be necessary. For Plato the world was made; it requires an intelligent, wise maker; it is ruled by a wise and loving providence. This requires a person, and in the Demiurge, Plato provides this person.

Thus we have in Plato many of the necessary elements of what for the Christian would be a sound natural theology.

And if we add his eloquent words about God as the cause of all good and nowise of evil (e.g. *Timaeus* 42 D; *Republic* 380 B; *Laws* 903) and about the vital importance of virtue as likeness to God (e.g. *Theaetetus* 176 ff.; *Laws* 716 C) and the rewards and punishments of the future life (e.g. *Republic* 612 ff.), the sketch is nearly complete. It must be confessed, however, that though a good case could be made out for the view that Plato held the existence of one supreme and unique God, it is not at all clear that he held one transcendent God in the full Christian sense, that is, one infinite God, essentially different in nature from all else. On the contrary, provided that it is safely established that intelligent soul of some kind is the efficient cause of the movement and intelligibility of the universe, Plato seems in many places quite willing to allow that there might be a number of such souls, all of which he is willing to call 'God'; so that 'God' and 'gods' may be found with about equal frequency in the pages of Plato. But at the same time the gods inferior to the Demiurge are described in the *Timaeus* as themselves dependent on the Demiurge for their existence, so that they would be roughly equivalent to angels in Christian theology; in fact, the way Plato describes the nature of these 'created gods' is strikingly similar to the way St Thomas describes the nature of the angels. It only remains to add that Plato, like all the Greeks before Christ, did not arrive at the idea of creation in the full sense. He postulates a 'receptacle' of creative activity, a formless matter, as we should probably interpret his words.

Aristotle was a pupil of Plato, and though he was saturated with his master's teaching, his was a remarkably original mind; and he criticized Plato's system very thoroughly, and in particular rejected the whole idea of a separate world of immaterial Forms or Ideas. To that extent he weakened his position when it came to explaining the ultimate intelligibility of the world. God, for Aristotle, is living, immaterial, unchangeable, pure thought. But this God has not available any pattern-ideas of the world. He does not think of the world: that, thought Aristotle, would be unbecoming in a Being so exalted. His life is the supremely blessed contemplation of Himself. Yet though he does not think of the world, this God is in another sense the cause of the order of the world. The world has an unconscious aspiration to be like God: God draws it as the object of its desire. But how can an unconscious world be drawn, and desire? Strictly speaking, it cannot. We may, of course, say that things have their own natures, and that these natures tend to their own good, and this is quite true. But if the world is not conscious and God is not conscious of the world, something essential has been missed out. Aristotle is one of the foremost upholders of the doctrine that the world is not due to chance; that it is due to purpose, as much as human activity is. Yet there cannot be true purpose without consciousness; nor, ultimately, can there be intelligible order. Aristotle's view that the world unconsciously aspires towards God and thus perfects itself would seem to be a relic of the view that came spontaneously to the Greeks, that the whole universe is one big living thing.

On the credit side we have, then, in Aristotle a God who is pure thought, spiritual, unchangeable, the cause of the movement and perfection of the world. On the other hand, this God does not set the world in order by thinking about it; there is no divine providence for the world in that sense. Nor is God, for Aristotle, *infinite* spirit. The fact is that Aristotle had the type of mind which tends to withhold judgment on anything far removed from our observation. He says comparatively little about God except for a few notable

passages. He seems afraid to commit himself on such difficult matters, even though they were the logical outcome
and crown of his metaphysical system. (He has still less to
say, and that little very obscure, about the immortality of
the soul.) Another curious feature about Aristotle's conclusions about God is that while in some passages he describes,
and gives definite reasons for preferring, a unique Unmoved
Mover or God, in other passages he concludes that there
must be as many unmoved movers as there are separate
heavenly spheres requiring to be moved. The astronomy of
the times postulated fifty-five or forty-seven heavenly
spheres; hence Aristotle concludes that there must be that
many unmoved movers each with the same characteristics.
But the difficulties involved in this plurality, even on
Aristotle's own metaphysical principles—and he notices
some of the difficulties himself—are so obvious that one can
only conclude that he intended to return to the problem;
and that meanwhile, not knowing what to say, he said
nothing.

In the same stream of thought some centuries later,
Plotinus, almost the last of the great Greek philosophers,
produced a new and very remarkable synthesis. In briefest
outline it is as follows. The ultimate reality, God in the
highest sense, is called the One, and sometimes also the
Good. Plotinus is identifying God with Plato's Form of the
Good. The One is the source of all things. Plotinus stresses
the utter transcendence of God, that is, the fact that all
other things are incommensurable with God. From this he
concludes that God is beyond our thought and understanding; that the nature of God Himself is not thought, but
beyond thought; not consciousness, but beyond consciousness; not being, but beyond being. The transcendence of
God is a fact, as will be explained in Part Two of this essay.

Plotinus in his explanation is in danger of overstressing the negative side, of exaggerating the unknowability of God.

From the infinite, transcendent One descends a hierarchy of 'emanations' in the order: Mind; Soul (from which are derived the 'soul of the world' and individual human souls); and lastly Matter. Emanation is a process like the streaming of light from the sun. It makes no difference at all to the One; it is a necessary process, not freely chosen by the One. It is a flowing from the substance of the One which does not deprive the One of anything. The first emanation, Mind, is eternal thought, knowing both the One and itself, and containing in a unity the whole Platonic world of Forms or Ideas, save for the original Form of the Good. This Mind is equated by Plotinus with Plato's Demiurge or Fashioner of the world. Thus Plotinus has united Plato's world of Forms with the Demiurge at a stage lower than the ultimate One; yet so closely connected with the One that we may say that the first emanation of the One is divine Mind and, in a broad sense, creator. From Mind emanates Soul, which is partly independent of the world and partly descends to provide the soul of the world and the souls of individual men, by a sort of unity-in-division. Human souls pre-existed in this great Soul before birth, and are individually immortal. Their presence in human bodies is described as a 'fall' which we have to correct by ridding our minds and desires of earthly objects and aspiring towards reunion through Soul with Mind and ultimately with the One—a union of contemplation which does not destroy the soul's individuality. The last emanation is Matter; with Matter, light shades off into darkness. Matter makes evil possible, but in a negative way, by obscuring the light that descends from the One.

It is to be noted that in general, for the Greek mind, *theos* (God) and *theios* (divine) had not the firm and distinct meaning which they have in Christian philosophy and theology. 'God' tended to shade off gradually into what is not God; and each philosopher has to be examined carefully if we want to determine what exactly 'God' and 'divine' meant for him. One may compare the loose use of 'divine' in modern literature.

The system of Plotinus greatly influenced St Augustine, and on the whole it seems to be the nearest ancient Greek approach to the Christian conception of God. At first sight it is a system that has the appearance of pantheism, that is, the doctrine that everything is either the same thing as God or at least has the same nature as God. But that was certainly not Plotinus's intention, whatever the logic of the situation might seem to require. Mankind, according to Plotinus, must work out their salvation through turning from material things and cultivating virtue and contemplating God. Ultimate happiness is the ecstatic vision of God, a vision which, Plotinus claimed, could be achieved even in this life by purified souls.

Early Christian theologians were not slow to see in Plotinus's first emanation, Mind, a similarity to the Second Person of the Blessed Trinity, 'through Whom all things were made', the Word of God, containing the Ideas of God, the archetypes of all created and creatable things. The differences, however, are equally obvious. Mind, for Plotinus, is lower than the One; the Christian Word of God is in no sense lower than the Father. Again, for the Christian creation is 'out of nothing' by the free will of God, not, as for Plotinus, a necessary emanation from the very substance of God. Lastly, God for the Christian is Himself pure thought, consciousness, will, goodness; He is not 'beyond' these things in the sense that they cannot be truly predicated of Him, but only in the sense that He is not finite, but infinite being, thought, will, unity, goodness, truth. We can only clearly understand these qualities of being, so to call them, in their finite manifestations; yet their infinite possession by God does not contradict the idea we have of them. This situation provides what has always been regarded as one of the main problems of natural theology: in what sense can we know God? I deal with it in Part Two of this essay.

Side by side with the Platonic-Aristotelean stream of thought in Greek philosophy there are several other and quite different streams, chiefly two, the Stoics and the Epicureans. There were also the Cynics, the short-lived Cyrenaic sect, the Pythagoreans and the Sceptics. It will be sufficient to consider here the first two, Stoics and Epicureans, with a brief glance at the Pythagoreans.

The Stoics were founded by Zeno of Citium in Cyprus (there were several other Greek philosophers named Zeno) about 300 B.C. Whereas Plato and Aristotle had confidently admitted the existence of incorporeal, immaterial, spiritual reality, the Stoics held that all reality is corporeal. For them the soul is material; and the whole universe is made up of two principles, both material, viz., Matter and Reason. Reason is God and 'is eternal and fashions each thing throughout the whole of matter'.[1] Thus God is in things: He is something like what Aristotle would have called the form, or as it were the soul of things, as distinct from their matter. God is body, but body of a specially pure and refined sort with, in practice, all the characteristics and functions of mind. 'Chrysippus and Zeno also say that God is the principle of all things; that He is a body of the purest kind; and

---

[1] Diogenes Laertius, vii, 134.

that His providence pervades everything.'[1] This is nominally materialism and pantheism; yet in practice it is made into a strongly religious philosophy with great emphasis on the importance of virtue and of 'living according to nature', that is, according to Reason or God, and with a feeling for the goodness and all-pervasiveness of divine providence which at its best expresses itself in terms of noble piety. For the Stoics, God's operation in the universe, virtuous, just and benevolent, is the same as Fate. To resign oneself to it and pursue virtue in spite of all seeming hardships, is to achieve human happiness.

Thus in spite of its materialistic principles the Stoic philosophy has features which have a large measure of truth in them; and Stoicism was much admired by early Christian philosophers. It should not cause surprise that the distinction between material and immaterial is blurred. It is not an easy distinction for the human mind to grasp; and, though there were learned Stoics who developed an advanced physical philosophy, they were not, on the whole, metaphysically-minded. Some Stoics tried hard to defend free will, at least in a restricted sense, but their defence satisfied few save themselves. Indeed, in a strictly materialistic philosophy, free will is impossible. As for immortality, some Stoics held that the souls of men survive after death until a periodic 'conflagration of the universe'; others held that only the souls of good men survive. Marcus Aurelius, one of the last of the great Stoics, thought there might be survival after death, but felt no solid assurance on the point.

Another of the great Greek systems is the materialist atomism of Epicurus, who also lived about 300 B.C., and whose system was reaffirmed some 250 years later in immortal verse in Lucretius's *De Rerum Natura, On the*

---

[1] Hippolytus, *Philosophumena*, 21, 1.

Nature of Things. Epicurus' mind is surprisingly modern in quite a number of ways. His chief aim is to rid men of superstitious fear by defending the view that such gods as there are take no interest whatever in men; that all that exists, gods included, is made up of atoms and empty space; and that there is no after-life for men. There is something of the psychoanalyst about Epicurus's approach: 'Our life's one need is to be free from alarms.' He stresses strongly the evidence of the senses as the criterion of truth: all error comes from mixing opinion about what is not evident with direct apprehension of what is evident. In order to explain motion, he postulates empty space—which is not apprehended by the senses. Further, the existence of individual atoms, and the qualities he assigns to them, are conclusions of reason, not something perceived by the senses. Pleasure and pain—those of refined and cultured men—are the criterion of good and bad. To explain free will, Epicurus postulated a slight and unpredictable deviation of atoms in the path of their movement: a theory which bears some resemblance to Heisenberg's Uncertainty Principle, which in recent years has been appealed to, quite mistakenly, to explain the possibility of free will. For Epicurus the world is formed by purely chance-movement of atoms in empty space, in a way that recalls the suggestion in Hume of material particles 'trying every possible order and position', and the apparent assumption of some modern scientists that by adding evolution to the chance-theory, the origin and development of the universe is easily explained. Finally, for Epicurus there is not one world, but an infinite number of worlds of various shapes.

It might have seemed that Epicurus would be the last person to believe in any kind of divinities, yet he does hold the existence of immortal gods. 'Epicurus presents us with gods whom light and wind can pass through, living in the space between two worlds, as it were between two sacred groves.'[1] These gods are in human form, not perceptible to the senses but only to the mind, on account of the tenuousness of the particles of which they are made. As has been said, they take no interest whatever in this world or in human affairs. One reason given by Lucretius why the world cannot be the work of gods is that it is *tanta praedita culpa*—so imperfect.

The Pythagoreans were an important philosophical school founded before 500 B.C. by Pythagoras of Croton in S. Italy. After about two centuries of more or less vigorous life followed by a period of eclipse, the school revived in Roman times about the first century B.C. There is a good deal of scattered information about the early Pythagoreans, but it is difficult to combine it into a coherent historical or philosophical picture. It is clear, however, that Pythagoreanism was a way of life with two tracks, religion and philosophy. In religion they held the transmigration of souls, and aimed at purification of the soul by ascetic and ritual practices; and though they had apparently no developed theology, there was at least this amount of correlation between religion and philosophy, that the study of the principles of music and mathematics was thought to help in purifying the soul. In philosophy they held that everything in the world may be explained by numbers, which were at first thought of spatially, like dots on a dice. Numerical ratios were found to exist in the basic intervals of the musical scale, and imagined to exist in the behaviour of the heavenly bodies, in the parts of the soul, in the soul as a harmony of the body, and even the different virtues were each assigned their number. The theory was no doubt due to the surmise,

[1] Cicero, *De Divinatione*, II, 40.

amply justified in the light of modern science, that the structure of material things can be expressed in precise mathematical terms; and also, it would seem, to the feeling that what appears to explain the visible world so well might be at least a good clue to the understanding of the invisible world, the world of the spirit and of religion. Music, a main preoccupation of the Pythagoreans, may have provided a tempting link between the two worlds. This may be thought of as a point of special significance in the Pythagoreans, that with them for the first time in Western philosophy, the visible and invisible worlds were recognized as distinct, and brought together with some attempt at correlation. Such a situation might develop in various ways. A philosopher might attempt to reduce the invisible world, the world of the soul and of religion, to the clear and distinct terms of mathematics. If he came to realize that this cannot be done, he might develop a theory of knowledge capable of covering both worlds, as Plato attempted to do. Or he might conclude that any apparent reality that cannot be expressed with mathematical clearness and distinctness, was an appearance only, and could be discounted without loss. Thus in the Western world, the rise and development of physical science has produced in some types of mind an ever-growing feeling that the categories and methods of physical science should be the categories and methods of all thought. Or finally, those who found themselves unable to formulate any correlation between knowledge of the visible and knowledge of the invisible worlds, might conclude that the world of the soul and of religion is a non-rational world which may be accepted as self-authenticating without the need or the possibility of further explanation; and this has been for some centuries the tendency of certain non-Catholic defenders of religion.

I pass now to a brief sketch of the mediaeval and modern periods, indicating the chief landmarks in the history of natural theology, and the chief philosophical rivals that Thomist natural theology has had to meet.

In philosophy St Augustine was basically a Platonist, and St Augustine's mind dominated Christian philosophy for eight hundred years until Aristotle was rediscovered and assimilated about the time of St Thomas. This historical fact explains St Thomas's great respect for the Augustinian tradition, even when it was being largely supplemented. In fact, it appears at times that St Thomas, like Aristotle, was more of a Platonist than perhaps he realized. The same association, at times uneasy, between the two philosophies, is quite evident in some departments of scholastic philosophy at the present day. The possibilities of synthesis have not yet been fully worked out, and hold out hopes of fresh advances.

St Augustine, then, offering reasons for the existence of God at the level of philosophy, argues like St Thomas from the need of postulating a first efficient cause; from the contingence of the world to a necessary or non-contingent being; and from the order of nature to a mind directing it. But he likes best his Platonic argument from the 'eternity' and 'necessity' of truth. He was greatly impressed by the fact that mathematical truths, for example, are not something which a man invents for himself, but something he finds in possession, something he must submit to, something he cannot change, something which seems to outlive any man and all men. Such truths thus have a certain necessity and eternity, and this, Augustine concludes, leads the mind up by immediate ascent to God, who is original and subsistent Truth, Necessity and Eternity. Augustine thought further that we could not see the necessity of these truths if our minds were not specially illuminated for this purpose by God. This, no doubt, any Christian might admit in some sense, in so far as minds, and the intelligibility of things, depend ultimately, and also immediately, on God. But, unlike St Augustine, St Thomas did not see any need for a special extrinsic illumination, and held that the mind of its own nature sees the necessity of necessary truths.

A sample of an Augustinian argument from contingence, that is, from the insufficiency detected in some aspect of finite being, is the following, in which Augustine neatly shows the contingence of all that is subject to temporal succession. He argues thus: That is contingent of which all the parts are contingent; but the parts of successive, temporal existence are all contingent: for the past no longer exists; the present will soon not exist; and the future does not yet exist. From this he concludes that existence in time is a continual becoming and passing away, dependent at every moment on the creative activity of God. Such a process of thought depends, no doubt, on the nature and significance of time, but rightly interpreted it could be for the Thomist a perfectly valid argument.

Other forms of argument of the Platonic type are to be found frequently in the Middle Ages—arguments from diversity to original Unity; from the imperfect and finite to the perfect and infinite; from degrees of truth to subsistent Truth, and so on. In judging of these forms of argument at this period, one should remember two things: first, that even if one is not disposed to accept the basically Platonic principle on which they rest—the principle, namely, that our universal concepts point *immediately* to the existence of eternal, spiritual archetypes, patterns or exemplars—still, the *psychological* difference between such a principle and the different principle of detecting contingence in all finiteness, and making this the starting-point for an argument based on efficient causality, is not great. The second thing to remember is that at this period a showing of the existence of God is more likely to be rather an analysis of what is already accepted as true than it could afford to be today when made available to those who doubt or deny the existence of God. This last remark applies also, and especially, to St Anselm's famous Ontological Argument (cf. Part Three, 7, 2.) which was expounded by a number of leading schoolmen of the thirteenth century and accepted by some of them, but rejected by St Thomas. And even if it is held that its medieval defenders thought the argument could stand on its own feet, they erred in the respectable company of Descartes, Spinoza, Leibniz and Hegel.

The modern age in philosophy, when philosophy began to be more and more independent of scholasticism, is usually dated from Descartes (d. 1650), a Catholic educated in the scholastic tradition, who tried to work out his own system independently of what he had been taught. He argues to the existence of God from the idea we have of the infinite, which idea, he thought, could only be produced in us by God. He further uses the idea of the infinite in a version of the Ontological Argument, arguing that the idea of the infinite contains the idea of existence, and that therefore God exists.

From Descartes's philosophy were derived two unacceptable doctrines of the Oratorian priest Malebranche (d. 1715), namely, *Occasionalism*, the theory that God is the only agent and that finite things do not really produce effects; and *Ontologism* (though not under that name), the theory that human knowledge involves direct intuition into the mind of God.

Spinoza (d. 1677), who belonged to a Jewish family

settled in Holland, held a pantheistic doctrine somewhat like that of the Stoics: there exists only one substance, an impersonal absolute, God, from which all else results by necessary derivation, and with which all else is in a way identified. Men are not independent substances; finite things are determined in their being and in their activity; and man's only freedom is freedom to recognize this situation and accept it.

Leibniz (d. 1716), a Protestant, proposed a new form of the Ontological Argument: If God is possible, He exists; but He is possible; therefore He exists. Leibniz also proves the existence of God from the necessity of postulating a first non-contingent cause of contingent things, and is also famous for a thoroughgoing philosophic Optimism, holding that God is morally obliged to produce the best of all possible worlds. Individual evils, he maintains, all co-operate in the end to the production of the highest possible created good.

In the eighteenth century some philosophers defended Deism, the doctrine that all that need be known about God and about man's relations to Him can be known easily from a consideration of the natural world, and that any other alleged divine revelation cannot add anything of importance to this. But on the nature of God and His causality in the world the Deists differed among themselves.

In the same century a most important name is that of Hume (d. 1776), who prepared the way for sceptical conclusions about what are called the principles of reason, notably that of causality. For Hume, causes and effects, and the principle of causality, though they are matters of natural belief without which life would be impossible, cannot be justified philosophically. The principle of causality, that every new event must have a cause, is neither self-evident nor demonstrable; and the necessity of a cause which we feel is explained through habit and association of ideas.

In the late eighteenth and early nineteenth centuries, besides a number of lesser but not inconsiderable trends, four main lines of thought may be distinguished:

(1) The revolutionary Critical Philosophy of Immanuel Kant has had, and continues to have, enormous influence not least in the sphere of religion. His position with regard to the existence of God is stated and criticized in some detail in later sections (Part Three, 7, 5; 8, 10). Here it will be sufficient to mention that as a consequence of his theory of knowledge he rejects the arguments of the speculative reason for the existence of God, in particular the Ontological, Cosmological and Teleological arguments. But he accepts the existence of God as a 'postulate of the practical reason', i.e. as something inescapably bound up with the requirements of the moral order. Kant concludes, ironically enough in the light of his subsequent influence: 'The possibility (of the postulates of the practical reason) can never be penetrated by the human mind; but at the same time, no sophistry will ever destroy even the simplest man's conviction that they are true.'

(2) In the nineteenth century in Germany, and later in England, the philosophy of Kant was developed in the direction of Idealism, the theory that tends to reduce all reality to mind or mental content. Absolute Idealism finds the absolute and ultimate reality in a personal, or more usually an impersonal, Mind or Idea, evolving in such a way as to produce finite thought by which the universal Mind attains consciousness. Schopenhauer was an Idealist of a different kind. For him reality is Will, which evolves at first unconsciously and then at a certain stage acquires consciousness. This consciousness is painful, because Will is

tension and effort, so much so that conscious will produces the worst of all possible worlds from which we should try to escape by detachment of the kind advocated by Buddhism.

(3) Positivism. Auguste Comte (d. 1857) propounded a theory which has had great influence. He distinguishes three stages in the evolution of human thought: (i) the *theological* stage, in which everything was explained in terms of divine powers or gods which were, in fact, according to Comte, the forces of nature personified; (ii) the *metaphysical* stage in which reality was explained in terms of such metaphysical notions as substance and cause, and these notions were used to prove the existence of the Absolute or God; and (iii) the *positive* stage, in which men admit only the facts of experience, so as to be able to control nature. There is no God, Comte maintains, except mankind.[1]

(4) Some philosophers, especially since the eighteenth century, have maintained that religion has a truth of its own which is known by immediate experience only, and is not known or controlled by reason. Important names in this connection are those of Jacoby (d. 1819), Schleiermacher (d. 1834) and Ritschl (d. 1889). The theory received fresh impetus at the beginning of the present century from Modernism, and still has some influence in non-Catholic religious philosophy at the present day. I deal with the subject at some length in the Third Part of this essay.

In the nineteenth century the following are some of the more important theories. It is recorded of St Paul (*Acts* xvii, 23) that he saw in Athens an altar dedicated 'to the unknown God', and the Greek word there used for 'unknown'

[1] Etienne Gilson wrote in 1941 that the problem of God in contemporary philosophy was wholly dominated by the thought of Kant and Comte. cf. E. Gilson, *God and Philosophy*, IV.

(*agnostos*) suggested to T. H. Huxley in 1869 [1] the word
'agnostic' to describe the view that we do not and cannot
know whether there is a God as an immaterial first cause of
the visible universe, or anything about an immaterial world
beyond this world. Agnosticism is thus a label for a doctrine
for which Hume paved the way—if he did not actually hold
it—by throwing doubt on all that is not available to the
senses.

Traditionalism was a theory defended by certain Catholics, chiefly of the Louvain school, that no truth about God
can be known with certainty from natural reason, but only
from divine or human faith helped by tradition. The theory
has also a mitigated form which claims that human reason
can prove things about God after they have been accepted
by faith or from tradition but not before.

The view that God can only be finite was defended by
Renouvier (d. 1903), the founder of the Neo-Critical school
which revived and developed the philosophy of Kant.
Similarly for *Pragmatism* as represented, e.g., by William
James (d. 1910) 'God' is that which seems to fulfil the dif-
erent or even contradictory spiritual needs of different
types of men; something of spiritual value in the subconscious life; but to claim further knowledge of it is to
indulge in hypothetical 'over-belief'.

The Sociological school of Durkheim (d. 1917) explained
the idea of God as the personification of the pressure and
authority of human society on men.

A contemporary theory of Lutheran inspiration, which
rejects or greatly depreciates natural theology, is the
Dialectical Theology of Barth and Tillich. This theory sees

---

[1] According to the ear-witness account of R. H. Hutton. Huxley
himself in *Collected Essays* gives a somewhat different derivation of
'agnostic'.

Christian faith as essentially the affirmation of truths which fly in the face of reason, which can never be reconciled with reason, yet are revealed by God in Holy Scripture and assented to by the believer under the guidance of the Holy Spirit. Barth would reject natural theology outright as being an impious attempt to explain God, whereas God is the 'wholly Other', wholly beyond the range of the human mind. More recently Tillich has shown himself disposed to allow that natural theology can be not altogether without value in its positive statements about God, though he himself prefers to stress the negative side, God's unknowability; and both Barth and Tillich are obliged to use in practice the analogy of being they reject in theory.

At the present time Logical Analysts quite rightly invite religious and metaphysical philosophers to make clear what their statements mean, and what sort of logic their discourse follows. Philosophers of religion in this country attempt to do this in various ways, for the most part not close to the Thomist way.

Throughout the modern period the philosophy of St Thomas was taught in most Catholic seminaries, but until comparatively recently in an historically uncritical form. By the first part of the nineteenth century, Thomism as a living philosophy was at a low ebb; but in the second half of the century it was revived, and has been enriched by the labours of philosophers of international repute, and overhauled from the historical point of view by eminent scholars in both Europe and America. Today the respectability of Thomism as a philosophy is not questioned by those who know it well.

2

Natural Theology and Revelation

THIS section is necessary to provide part of the answer to the question: What is Thomist natural theology? The problem is obvious enough. Bertrand Russell remarks in connection with St Augustine, that for Augustine the answers to philosophical problems were known in advance from revelation, so that he was not really doing philosophy at all. For reasons I shall give presently, I do not think this verdict does full justice to the situation.

For the Catholic philosopher, the relation between natural theology and revelation is briefly as follows. The human reason is able, by its natural exercise, to know with certainty that God exists—a personal God, the beginning and end of all things and in particular of man—and to recognize the obligation of accepting God's claim on the human mind, will and heart. This is true of the human reason in general; but external circumstances, and mental and moral conditioning, may stand in the way in particular cases, making it difficult or even impossible, at least for a time, to recognize the existence and nature of God, and man's relations and obligations to Him. In fact, difficulties of one sort or another are so common that mankind as a whole need revelation in order to know with certainty those truths about God which the human mind can, absolutely speaking, acquire for itself without revelation. In this way, revelation is said to be not absolutely necessary, but morally necessary, where 'morally necessary' means necessary in order that the truth about God may be known 'by all men without difficulty, with unwavering certainty, and without admixture of error'.[1] Thus a man without philosophy who accepts revelation is able to hold truths about God on divine faith, that is, on the word of God revealing; and is able to hold the existence of God as a truth bound up with the recognition and acceptance of the Church as speaking with the voice of Christ, just as a person could have accepted Christ's claim to be God when He made it in person on earth. To see this situation as merely a logical puzzle would be a mistake. It is essentially a matter of person meeting Person, of man meeting Christ. I shall have a word more to say about the presence of Christ in the Church presently. Here I wish to say what happens to the believer who is also a philosopher. As a believer he is in the same position as any other; and his being a Catholic makes a difference to his philosophy. There is a dependence of his philosophy on his faith, but it is a negative, not a positive dependence. The Catholic does not import into his philosophy any premise or conclusion from his faith; but he knows there are conclusions in philosophy which would be untrue because they would contradict his faith. Apart from this, he is free to speculate, and his field is a wide one. Some would hold that this is not doing philosophy at all; that philosophy must be completely free from even negative dependence on religious faith. But the Catholic philosopher claims to expound and defend all his positions like any other philosopher on the

---

[1] Vatican Council, Constitutio Dogmatica de Fide Catholica, cap. 2, de Revelatione (ut . . . ab omnibus expedite, firma certitudine et nullo admixto errore cognosci possint).

ground of reason alone. And even if what he is doing were not philosophy, it could not be said that it is not reasonable. Every Catholic, philosopher or not, has complete certainty that the Church is what she claims to be, and he thereupon believes what the Church teaches, as God's revelation if it is taught as revealed truth, and with the appropriate quality of assent if it is taught as a more or less close, more or less certain, consequence of revelation. To give this assent, the grace of God is as a matter of fact necessary; but so far as the recognition of the Church is concerned, this grace does not supersede reason but only enlightens it.

For the non-religious philosopher, the centre of gravity in matters of certitude may be philosophy itself. This is quite reasonable in many departments of thought. For the Catholic, the centre of gravity in matters of religious certitude is his faith. He knows that Christ is God and that He lives and speaks in His Church; that that is the way God has provided for men. Such complete and universal certainty about the essentials of revelation is not available to the non-Catholic. A common attitude is perhaps that of a countryman of my acquaintance. 'There are two things a man can never be sure about—politics and religion.' The non-religious philosopher often thinks of the Catholic's point of view as an irrational hangover from less enlightened times; the Catholic sees his faith as the incomparable source of light.

I have said that the Catholic recognizes Christ in the Church, and that his faith is based on the meeting of person with Person. The Church is said in theological language to be the Mystical Body of Christ because of its union with Christ by grace, which is a sharing of the life of God so close as to unite the members to one another and with God as the cells are united in a living body. So the Catholic tends to see Christ everywhere in the Church in a sort of kaleidoscopic multiplicity in unity: Christ in the whole Church, Christ in each member, Christ in a special way in the saints, in priests, in bishops, in the Pope as the Vicar of Christ; Christ in the sacraments, and above all in the Holy Eucharist, whose influence, even in its external manifestations, must be one of the biggest prodigies in the history of mankind.

It is not easy to present to non-Catholics what, in a general way, it feels like to be a Catholic. One may mention one or two points. The first is that the content of faith, while it always remains faith and is not vision, is, psychologically speaking, in the daily life of the practising believer, remarkably like vision. It is rather like facts one has acquired about a strange country one hopes one day to visit. Not at all like standing blindfold on the edge of a cliff and being told, 'Jump, it will be all right'; much more like seeing one's way and walking in it. Phrases like 'the venture of faith' sound slightly odd to the Catholic. He is much more at home with words like the following from a Collect prayer: ' . . . grant that we may show forth in our works that which through faith shines (*fulget*, blazes, almost) in our minds'.[1] The same word comes in the great Passiontide hymn, the *Vexilla Regis*: *fulget Crucis mysterium*—the mystery of the Cross is all aglow with light. The supernatural mysteries of revelation are not dark, but luminous; we cannot penetrate them for their depth of light; but we can look at them and be absorbed by them, as we can look at the sky or the sea. But to the believer it is not just a matter of believing things, but of loving a Person. The palpable parts of this life are astonishing enough. Christianity is sometimes spoken of as failing or dying. This may sound

[1] ' . . . *concede ut* . . . *id in opere exhibeamus quod per eam* (*fidem*) *fulget in mente*'.—Collect prayer of the Mass for the feast of B. Julian Maunoir.

strange to the Catholic. He has only to look as far as the nearest parish church, or into his own life, to know that the Church is very much alive, and the giver of life. Knowing and loving Christ in His Church, he has no need of reasons. Yet he knows that life incorporated in Christ's Church is the potential source of reasons, very powerful even taken singly. He may reflect, for instance, that if there were something false at the heart of prayer, some at least of those who give themselves wholeheartedly to prayer would sooner or later find it, but that this never happens; and that while very many thousands of people have prayed themselves into the Catholic Church, those who leave the Church do not do so because they are men of prayer.

There is in the modern mind a distrust of big institutions and centralized authorities. The human mind, once such a proud boast, is now widely thought to be very much in the dark. But that only makes the ordinary man all the more determined to see for himself what is going on. He knows what happens under his eyes, and he knows where the shoe pinches. For him, centralized authorities are not only dark because human, but out of reach and rather sinister. The Catholic does not have that kind of feeling about the Church. For him the Church is divine first and human second; and even in practice there is no real difficulty in distinguishing the two factors. The purely human side may arouse in him the same feelings as do purely human elements anywhere else. But when the Church speaks with full authority, it is not men who speak, but God through men.

Finally, being a Catholic does not mean thinking everyone else is completely wrong. Those non-Catholics who claim to follow Christ he sees as people who have accepted Christ, but not the whole Christ; as like disciples who have mistakenly gone off preaching Christ independently of the

Apostles. They may be preaching and practising much that is true, but they are preaching and practising one thing that is not true. And for that, the Catholic holds, they have not Christ's approval.

What, then, is Thomist natural theology in the whole context of human life? Is it true that because of its negative dependence on revelation it is not genuine philosophy at all? It seems to me that in this matter any circumspect philosopher would want to do a good deal of heart-searching before he cast the first stone. No doubt men can come to modify their views through doing philosophy. But on the whole, it seems that it would be nearer the mark to say that men's conclusions in philosophy are largely conditioned by whatever convictions they possess independently of philosophy. How otherwise account for so much diversity? If they are not aware of having any convictions before they take to philosophy, they may do philosophy in the hope of finding some. Or they may think of philosophy as simply a way of clarifying ordinary ways of thinking, and of detecting illusions. In the latter case they will be assuming, reasonably enough, that they may have illusions to detect. But it would be unreal to take it for granted that independently of philosophy a man may not have certainties which he knows are not illusions, especially about persons and basic loyalties. There is not such a radical cleavage between philosophy and life. Philosophy is only careful thinking. A man's conclusions in philosophy are only an attempt to save the appearances as they appear to him after careful scrutiny. How they appear after careful scrutiny is not just the result of a new and objective screening called philosophy. In philosophy, no less than in ordinary life, one man's meat is another man's poison.

Why, then, Thomist philosophy? What is meant by

calling Thomist philosophy the official philosophy of the Catholic Church? Only this, that the Church has declared that the philosophy of St Thomas is her chosen way of expressing, in the framework of reason, the world-view that is implied by being a Catholic. This does not mean that Thomism is the only possible philosophy. It is *a* philosophy, and I think it is a good one; and its basic principles are those of philosophers who knew nothing of revelation. But it may be said to be incomplete, and capable of fresh perspectives and developments. It is not infallible, and it contains much that is uncertain. There is a great deal of controversy amongst philosophers who claim the name of Thomist. The Church has defined that the human reason is capable of finding out for itself that God exists; but it has not been defined that any particular proofs of the existence of God are absolutely valid, not even the Five Ways of St Thomas, though they have been given a general approval. There is, in fact, a whole library of literature on the meaning and force of the Five Ways. There are widely diverging interpretations. And not all scholastic philosophers accept the interpretations usually called Thomist. Suarez, for example, rejected one of the principles on which, according to the Thomist interpretation, the First Way rests.

Another point connected with reason and revelation is the re-statement which for historical reasons is today required of the relation between intellectual approaches to God and what is called religious experience. It will be evident from the sketch of religious philosophy since Descartes that, on the whole, religious philosophers outside the Catholic Church have come to rely much less on the ordinary working of the human mind, and much more on religious experience. The main reasons for this are traceable, directly or indirectly, to the Protestant Reformation. Then the attempt was made to dissolve external authority as the vehicle of divine revelation. With external authority gone, if a man finds himself unable to decide by the ordinary use of his mind, he will decide, if he decides at all, by consulting his feelings. After all, religious people may argue, cannot the Holy Spirit speak directly to each man? Is not the individual of ultimate importance to God, and has he not got individual needs? And what is surprising if the mind, so successful in natural science, should have proved to be the wrong instrument for acquiring religious enlightenment and certainty, especially since science seems to have become such a bugbear to religion? If God is unique and transcendent, what is surprising if the special instrument of religious enlightenment is also unique—a unique religious sense, of unmistakable quality, its own guarantee, something of which a man can be immediately certain, whatever other people may feel or say?

Of the insufficiency of religious experience simply by itself I deal in a later section. Here I only want to present the overall picture as the Catholic sees it. Religion is not for him a mere matter of feeling, and it is not natural theology; it is one thing only, the finding of Christ and the acceptance of Him on His own terms. And this, the Catholic holds, means the recognition and acceptance of the Church He founded, in which He lives, to which He gave the charge to teach all nations, to which He gave the keys of the kingdom of heaven, and to which He said, 'He that heareth you heareth me; and he that despiseth you despiseth me.' It would be a mistake to imagine that the Catholic makes light of religious experience, or does not have any. It is a matter of perspective. As a human phenomenon religious experience is for the Catholic something that either leads to or supervenes upon the recognition of religious truth from whatever source, reason or revelation; and revealed truth is to be recognized in a Person who is God as well as man, and who teaches men to whom He has given minds as well as feelings, but minds first; so that they are happy about God when they have got the truth about God from God Himself. The Catholic's personal relations with Christ, without sacrificing anything of their directness or individuality, are inseparable from life in the Church. As a personal relation, it is essentially similar to any other, and includes the normal factors of mind, will, heart and feelings. The feeling element as such, tends to be taken for granted by the Catholic, as it is taken for granted in any other sphere of healthy love. But it always had a place in his life at some stages, and even the memory of it can be a great help in reminding him that he belongs to a living, healthy, and above all a holy body. Based on these normal human principles, his spiritual life is as tranquil and unforced as the life of anyone who loves and knows that he is loved.

3

Some Principles of St Thomas's Philosophy

I T may be useful as part of the background to give some of the principles of St Thomas's philosophy. To elaborate these and defend them against the rival principles and theories which have been proposed since the time of Descartes, would be outside the scope of the present essay.

St Thomas's philosophy may be described as founded on that of Aristotle, and as being close to common sense. The world is seen as a unity of separate but interrelated things, existing independently of their being known by human minds. Some contemporary Thomists would prefer to see the *material* universe as so closely unified that it would be better regarded as one thing, not a number of separate things. This, however, would not apply to human minds which, for all their dependence on the material universe, on the body and on one another, must be regarded as essentially separate units.

St Thomas, following Aristotle, distinguishes between substance and accidents, the substance being what we mean by the thing as that which can exist on its own, and accidents being modifications of the thing, modifications which can only exist in the thing, not on their own. Thus the velocity of an arrow is not the arrow, and there cannot be velocity in the concrete without a thing which has it, though of course, velocity can be considered by itself in abstraction. How far what are called the accidents or properties of a thing can be taken away while the thing remains is another question, though evidently some of them can. The difference between thing and modification of thing is seen most clearly in our interior states, through observing that the self remains and can have sensations and thoughts and acts of will which come and go. Material things are understood in terms of substance and accidents on the analogy of what we find in ourselves. But it is only an analogy; the unity and independence of a person are much higher than those of a purely material thing. It must be admitted that our understanding of what we mean by 'thing' in the sense of material substance is limited. We have no intellectual intuition in the full sense into anything of our experience. But it is claimed that to retain the notion of 'thing' as 'that which can exist on its own', and as the dynamic, unifying source of accidents, properties and actions, is the only way to make sense of our internal experience, and the best way of making sense of external reality as it is presented to us.

Another way of viewing things is in terms of what they *are* and what they *can become*. These two factors in things are called act and potency; and the formulation and explanation of this division is one of Aristotle's chief titles to fame as a philosopher. The potency in this connection is passive potency, the thing's capacity not to act but to be acted upon. This division, though important and not always easy to apply, is close to common sense and need not detain us here. It may be mentioned that God is pure act, that is, infinite act, with no capacity for change, either to increase or to decrease. All finite things are compounded of act and potency, of what they are and their capacity to become different. Opposite to passive potency is active potency, the power not to be acted upon but to act, not to suffer change but to produce it. Active potency is in proportion to act, or actuality: the kinds of change a thing can produce depend on the kind of thing the agent is. Causality and the principle of causality are discussed at length in Part Three of this essay.

In material things, the division into act and potency includes the division into matter and form. Form is not just shape, and matter is not just matter as understood by science or common sense. Form is the factor in things which gives them their positive intelligibility; it describes the nature and qualities of the thing—iron, acorn, man; large, red, clever. Pure matter, or prime matter, as it is called, has no actuality of its own, but is the factor in material things which produces their characteristic limitations—existence in time and space, divisibility, capacity for change.

The human soul, an immaterial substance, is not essentially dependent on matter for its existence, and can exist apart from the human body. Yet the soul has natural dependence on matter for its operations; its knowledge, for example, begins with the senses, though it does not end with them.

Spiritual substance, including the human soul, has the power of self-determination called free will. This means that when the mind apprehends some object as good and choosable, it does so against a background of good in general, of good that may be greater than and less than that of the object apprehended; so that the will is able to choose anywhere within the range of possible good, and is not limited to the particular good that here and now presents itself. Some further account of free will is given in Part Two, section 6, 4, *God's concurrence with finite causes*. The fact of free will may be known from three considerations: first, from immediate consciousness; second, from the requirements of the moral order; and third, from the nature of the intellect, which sees particular good against the background of good in general, as has been said. But these three considerations are only three aspects of the same thing. It is impossible to understand free will if it is thought of in material terms, or if the imagination is allowed to take control with metaphors such as 'turning' this way and that. Free causality is understood by analogy with material causality, that is, by contrast with it. What belongs to matter because of its imperfection as matter is denied of spirit because of its perfection as spirit. This does not mean that our understanding of immaterial, free causality has no content. The content is that free will determines itself; and that to determine oneself is essentially greater perfection than to be determined by another. Free causality is often mistakenly thought to involve something uncaused, wild, erratic, irrational, or 'loose'. This is not so in the way supposed. Free will is not uncaused; the will causes itself to choose, determines itself to choose. The sufficient explanation of free choice is—apart from God's concurrence— the free will and choosable good; and it is neither necessary nor possible to look further for an explanation. This is not to say that the will is not influenced by external factors, but only that it is not determined by them. The only loose or irrational element in free choice is the choice of evil. Yet even here the apparent good chosen, and the deficient will that chooses, are all the explanation that can or need be given.

Human knowledge involves two essentially different though interrelated factors: sense and intellect. Animals have the first, not the second. The senses apprehend the material individual; the intellect finds and addresses itself to the universal in things, that by which things are alike. Sen-

sations and universal concepts are not things known, but
functions of knowledge, ways of knowing things. It is the
fundamental error of empiricism to suppose that there are
things called sense-data which are the direct objects of the
senses. The truth is that we see, and know, things, not colour-
patches and abstract concepts. All reality has something in
common, at least the fact that it either exists or could exist;
and metaphysics, as understood by the Thomist philosopher,
is simply the knowledge of what is implied by existence, and
knowledge of the most fundamental differences of things. If
we assume that God exists, then that which exists or could
exist includes three basic categories: (i) that which exists
of its own very nature—God; (ii) that which exists in dependence on God and with relations to other things, but otherwise on its own—substances; (iii) that which exists not on its
own but in essential dependence on substance—accidents.
Another chief division is that already mentioned between
pure act, God, and things which combine act and potentiality, i.e. all else besides God. All that exists or could exist
is available to the human understanding one way or another,
directly or indirectly. Thus metaphysics need not be thought
of as something very much in the air; it is rather something
down-to-earth. It is true that reflection on what is in this
world can lead the mind to see the necessity of what is not
part of this world. But this is a matter not to be undertaken,
or dismissed, lightly. It is in the hope of helping those who
are prepared to make the attempt that the following pages
have been written.

PART TWO

THE NATURE OF GOD

4

Some Divine Attributes

ANY showing of the existence of God concludes to a Being possessing some characteristic which belongs to God and to God alone, e.g. first cause, or necessary Being, or infinite Being. Any division between knowing *that* God is, and knowing *what* God is, is to some extent artificial; but it is convenient to make the infinity of God the link between the two parts.[1] Accordingly, the Third Part of this essay, showing God's existence, reaches the conclusion that God is infinite being; and the present part begins with an examination of what God's infinity means.

1. *The meaning of God's infinity*

God, we say, is the Being of infinite perfection, that is, of infinite greatness of being, or infinite intelligibility. Or, as is sometimes said, rather less aptly, God is infinite in all perfections.

Infinity is basic in any philosophical consideration of God.

[1] St Thomas frequently says that we can know *that* God is (*an est*) but not *what* God is (*quid est*); but that is a technical use of language, and means only that we cannot have a direct and adequate knowledge of the essence of God, but only an indirect, analogical knowledge.

Only God is infinite being; any finite being is not God.[1]

Historically, Christians, both teachers and taught, have found God's infinity an acceptable and intelligible notion. All understand that God must be infinite. No infinity, no God.

The ordinary intelligent Catholic brought up to think of God and pray to Him as infinite, finds the idea of infinite being, when he ponders on it, intelligible enough to start with, and mysterious when he begins to think it out. That is exactly as it should be. Infinite being is initially clear in its definition: it is being that is not finite, that has no limits. But it is mysterious when we try to think out what the definition amounts to.

People probably all begin by thinking of God's infinity as somehow like space—seemingly endless, always outstripping our thought. This may be called the frontal attack, the attempt to understand the infinite directly. It has its value, but it is not the only way available and is insufficient by itself. It might leave the impression that infinity issues in the indefinite, because it issues in what cannot be grasped clearly. Infinity, as has been said, is clear in one way and not clear in another. This special combination of clearness of definition and obscurity of content is a characteristic of analogical knowledge, the sort of knowledge we have of the immaterial and of God; and to that important topic I will turn presently. Meanwhile I leave the first and obvious description of infinity to suggest its own questions to the reader's mind.

Another definition of infinite being may seem more forbidding at first, but will be found more enlightening in the end. Infinite being is being that *transcends* the finite; that is,

[1] Theologically, a knowledge of God sufficient for salvation need not explicitly include infinity: in that context a confused knowledge is sufficient, that is, a knowledge which by any note sufficiently distinguishes God from what is not God.

the infinite is so great that the finite is *incommensurable* with it; or again, so that infinite being would not be increased by any finite addition.

This second formula lends itself to explanation on the following lines. The idea of transcendence can be scaled down to the proportion of our minds by considering the relation between a point and an area, say that of a circle. A point is a mathematical fiction, but it is intelligible. It is arrived at by supposing that which has position but no magnitude. Now compare the geometrical point with an area. They have something in common: they are both understood with reference to spatial position. But no multiplication of points will ever produce an area, or even a continuous line. An area *transcends* points, is incommensurable with them in the order of spatial magnitude.

This comparison, imperfect as it is in some ways, gives us, I believe, a useful clue to the understanding of infinite being. Just as a finite area transcends points in the order of spatial magnitude, so God's infinite being transcends all possible finite being. A point adds no length to a line, no area to a circle; finite being adds no being to the infinite being of God. This is not to say that finite being is nothing; it is finite being, just as a point is a point. But finite being is nothing in comparison with God, in the sense that God and finite being are not more being but only more entities.

Does this explanation claim to remove all difficulties? By no means. It is a clue only. If the spatial comparison is pressed, it might be thought that if there is infinite being, there is no 'room' for finite being—though to this one might reply that, compared with infinite being, finite being does not need any room. But leaving aside the spatial factor, it is a real question how the infinite and the finite can co-exist. The comparison does not claim to show how this is so. We

know that the infinite and the finite do co-exist by knowing that the infinite exists and that the finite exists, and that
they are adequately distinct; but we have no direct insight
into how this is possible, because we have no direct insight
into God. That is all that can be expected in this question and
in every question about God. The situation is always essentially
the same. The right answer always seems challenging and
attractive, difficult but not impossible. It can be shown that
certain things are so; one can try to remove misunderstandings; but the truths that can be established about God can
never be seen directly, because God can never be seen directly in this life.

It may be necessary to point out, at least to beginners,
that God's infinity has nothing whatever to do with space or
distance. God is not a being of infinite *size* in that sense; in
fact, size in a spatial sense contains an inherent imperfection—the imperfection of divisibility or lack of perfect
unity—which infinite extension would not remove but only
emphasize. Hence extension cannot be in God. Even God's
immensity and ubiquity, His presence in extended things, is
nothing like that. All the same it is useful to remember that
all perfection of being is understood by starting with size,
though a moment's reflection will show that it soon leaves
the region of size to enter that of quality or value. We say
that spirit has 'greater' perfection than matter; we speak of
a 'scale' of being and 'grades' of perfection, applying spatial
words beyond the spatial sphere even when we have denied
that spirit is material or spatial. Such is part of the analogical
or pointer-use of language which we are obliged to employ
when we speak of the immaterial.

Finally, God's infinity is not the infinity of the indefinitely expanding; nor is it anything else indefinite. In itself it
is as definite as a circle is to our minds, though with our

present limited way of knowing, we cannot get God's infinite definiteness, or definite infinity, into one clear concept.

What can be said about the content of this infinite being
of God? This in the first place, that it is infinite intellect.
Aristotle hit upon what may be usefully regarded as, with
infinity, the most basic attribute of God. For Aristotle, as for
St Thomas, God is pure intellect, pure thought. And infinite intellect, if properly analysed, can be shown, when
combined with the fact of creation, to contain all that can
be known about God by natural reason. The showing that
God is intellect will occupy us later.

2. *Analogical knowledge* is indirect knowledge; and particular
kinds of it are the sort of knowledge we have of the immaterial and of God. It is *indirect* knowledge: we have no
clear immediate insight into the nature of our own souls,
much less into the nature of God. It is knowledge that is a
mixture of clearness and obscurity, clear in its definitions,
obscure in the content of the definitions. Finally, it is knowledge that is made up of both positive and negative factors.

Analogy in its Greek original meant proportion. In proportion we compare one thing with another. In analogical
knowledge of the immaterial and of God, we understand
something we do not know directly by comparison with
something we do know directly. Usually when we compare
one thing with another, we know, or hope we shall eventually be able to know, both the things directly. But in the
case of God, of pure spirit, and even of our own spiritual
selves, we cannot know them directly and clearly at all in
this life. The method of description-by-comparison is used
by everybody all day long; but in analogical knowledge of
God the situation is quite special: first, because what is here
described is what can never be known directly in this life;

and secondly, because God is not mere spirit, but infinite spirit.

If we allow the existence of pure spirits as well as of God and of embodied human souls, the psychological foundation of the matter may be illustrated by a diagram. Here the

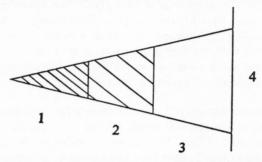

lowest division (marked 1) represents material things, stones, plants, animals; the next represents men, spirit embodied in matter; the third, finite pure spirit; and the last God, infinite spirit. According to St Thomas's theory of knowledge, which is largely based on that of Aristotle, a knower cannot know directly anything of greater perfection than himself. What a knower can know directly is called the *proportionate object* of his mind, that which his mind is big enough to grasp directly. The further foundation of the theory is that the knower becomes what he knows, in the sense that he receives and assimilates the perfection of the thing known, in so far as he knows it. Therefore we cannot know directly anything of essentially greater perfection than ourselves. Man, as embodied spirit, knows directly only material things and things compounded with matter—stones, plants, animals, himself.[1]

[1] The case of man's knowledge of himself needs more precising. We know a good deal about ourselves, but we have no direct intellectual intuition of the spiritual essence of the soul. This knowledge is not a

At various times in history there have been philosophers who have maintained one or other of two opposite errors: the first, that we can somehow know God's nature directly; the second, that we cannot know God at all, or that our knowledge of Him is purely negative. Between these extremes lies the doctrine of analogical knowledge. Let us examine it further.

I have already said that it is indirect knowledge. Further, it is knowledge that is produced by factors that are partly negative. God Himself, the reality towards which we point, is, of course, in Himself wholly positive; the words we use, and the corresponding thoughts in our minds, are partly negative and partly positive. The statement of the nature of God, in barest outline, contains three terms, 'being', 'not', 'finite'. Being is a positive term; not is negative; finite is partly negative in so far as it means being that goes up to a certain point, and *not* beyond it.

The question may be put, in what sense is the expression 'infinite being' informative? In reply it can be said in the first place that the words apply to God and to Him alone, and so distinguish Him from everything else. Next, on the common-sense level, to speak of being that is so great as to

---

matter of direct intuition but of abstraction and reflection. We have, of course, immediate awareness of ourselves at the level of the senses and the feelings, but this is not immediate insight of spirit by spirit. And again, we have insight into all sorts of intellectual truths; but these are not spiritual *things* existing in their own right, but abstractions. The question, too, remains how much insight we really have, by means of abstraction, into the natures of material things—stones, plants, animals. So far as such knowledge is clear, it is very sketchy, as St Thomas points out in *Contra Gentiles*, 4:1. The conclusion must be that we have to use analogical knowledge to a greater or lesser extent all the time not only about God and spiritual substance, but even about material things. It cannot be claimed, either, that we have any direct insight into the souls of others. We can, of course, build up, by the use of mind and senses, an intimate knowledge of others, as we can of ourselves; but so far as the souls of others are concerned, it is not direct.

be infinite, does seem to be informative. If we examine more closely how this is so, what the information consists of, it can be said that the information conveyed is not wholly negative. To say that God transcends the finite is to say that He is positively infinite. The content of this assertion is not in every way negative, even to our minds, i.e., it does not make God for us simply an unknown *X*. If God were for us simply an unknown *X*, then we could say anything at all about Him without patent absurdity. But we cannot do this : it is clear, for instance, that it would be untrue and absurd to say that God is made of stone. Our knowledge of God, imperfect as it is, controls our thoughts and language about Him rigorously. If it were no knowledge at all, but pure ignorance, this would not be so.

In what way, then, is the phrase 'infinite being' positively informative ? It is claimed that the phrase *is* positively informative, but in the unique way proper to analogical knowledge of the infinite, that is, indirectly informative. The factors of the expression 'infinite being' do not focus in our minds into one clear concept; but we judge that they do focus, beyond the range of our minds, in God Himself. Analogical knowledge, therefore, can never be clear and distinct as our knowledge of material things is clear and distinct.

This indeed is the essential point : analogical knowledge is not clear knowledge. On first acquaintance with the problem and its solution, the student is inclined to complain, 'Surely the job of philosophy is to make things clear. What sort of philosophy is this that tries to sell me obscurity as the answer to my problem ?' Or again, 'If I can know no particle of God exactly as He is, then I can know nothing at all about Him.' Exasperation of this kind is very natural, but patient pondering can dispel it.

First of all, it is the job of philosophy to make situations clear; and to make clear that this situation, our knowledge of infinite being, is unique. It is not the business of philosophy to perform the impossible feat of making our knowledge of God clear and distinct, but to make it clear why our knowledge of God cannot be clear, and to explain as well as possible what sort of knowledge we can have of Him.

Next, it is admitted that we do not know in any way the divine essence directly and just as it is. Analogical knowledge is imperfect knowledge of a special kind. Its imperfection does not consist in our knowing a little about God's essence as it is in itself, but not a great deal—as a person might know a little about mathematics but not a great deal; it is imperfect knowledge not in the sense of being small in quantity, but of being different in kind; a kind of knowledge that is entirely indirect, entirely comparative, made up of factors that are partly negative, which will not focus in our minds, but which point beyond the range of our minds to their object, to where they do focus into one, if one may use the expression, in God Himself. If we could understand God as He is in Himself, we should see what we cannot see at present, that God can be both definite and infinite; we should see that His infinity is in itself as clear and definite as a circle now is to our minds. Such is our understanding of God's infinity; to the Christian philosopher in his workshop, a perfectly workable and well-behaved concept; for all Christians in their thoughts and prayers, God Himself. No infinity, no God.

The contemporary school of logical Analysts are rendering a service to philosophy by inducing philosophers of all schools to examine more carefully the meaning of the words they use. This is all to the good. Any philosopher who is weak as a logical analyst will be weak as a philosopher. On the other hand, some logical analysts have a negative philosophy of their own. They doubt or deny the existence of God and of the immaterial, and those conclusions of reason—or some of them—which cannot be verified by the senses. This doctrine they recommend by trying to show that the objects of mind I have referred to are found, when closely examined, to have no meaning. Philosophers of this persuasion sometimes adopt the principle that what cannot be explained scientifically—that is, in the clear and distinct terms of physical science, logic or mathematics—cannot be explained at all. Physical science deals with what can be apprehended by the senses and measured. The position of these philosophers is, then, that either only material things exist, or, if non-material things do exist, they can make no sense for us. From one point of view one can sympathize with them. No one who has made any excursions in the field of learning can forget the unique thrill of the clear and distinct knowledge of science, mathematics and logic; of knowing that the field of study is entirely under one's control, and that though the search may be long and arduous, sooner or later the solution will come out in a neat, clean formula. Contrast, too, this clearness and distinctness, they would say, with the endless, inconclusive quarrels of the philosophers. Science deals with what I have described as the proportionate object of the human mind in this life—the things we can know directly, clearly, distinctly. It is excusable if, in the first flush of personal achievement in the scientific field, a man should be tempted to feel that what can be understood so clearly, so satisfyingly, is the only reality. Those who thus restrict reality would reject in principle analogical knowledge of God, of the immaterial, and of many other objects of mind defended by scholastic philosophers. Those in whom the sense of history is strong, and who do not equate progress in science with human progress, would hesitate before taking such a step. The possibility remains that positivism is an artificial system of choosing what is comparatively easy to understand, and saying the rest does not make sense; whereas the rest may be harder to understand through excess of intelligibility rather than through defect.

The question does, however, occur to any thinking person why knowledge of God is not easier to acquire. Apart from the obscuring of the intellect caused by the Fall of man, it would seem to be part of the essential tension of creature-hood that it should be so. Some tension there must inevitably be in every intellectual creature towards God in this life. Even the angels had the tension of finiteness; before they were granted the Beatific Vision their minds could not apprehend God directly, but only by means of finite infused species. Human creatures have the further disadvantage that the proportionate object of their minds is not even purely immaterial. We have to seek and find God in spite of these seeming disadvantages. That is part, perhaps the greater part, of our trial. It can be a painful thing; and if we had nothing but philosophy to help us, we should have far less help than God has been pleased to give us.

It may be wondered why nothing has been said in this section about Analogy of Attribution, whether intrinsic or extrinsic, and Analogy of Proportionality. The reason is that it has been my misfortune to find these frames of approach, as expounded by such of their patrons as I have read, not very enlightening in the present matter. On the other hand, in the distinct though allied question of the analogy of our concept of being, I find the Thomist application of Analogy of Proportionality a reasonable explanation.

3. *Infinite in all perfections?*

It is said, in the language of both prayer and philosophy, that God is infinite wisdom, infinite love, omnipotent, infinite justice, truth and goodness; and, from revelation at least, we attribute to Him infinite mercy. A number of rather obvious questions suggest themselves as a result. What is the meaning of these terms as applied to God? If the phrase 'infinite in all perfections' be admitted, how many perfections are all perfections? Further, if the nature of God is entirely simple, as it is, how can He contain all these different perfections, and each in an infinite degree? The attributes of God include also eternity, immensity, unity and simplicity. Are these on the same footing as wisdom, love and the others of that kind?

First, to clear the ground a little, I will state two conclusions at which we shall arrive:

(i) *There are certain perfections which are called pure perfections, and these are attributed to God.* Pure perfections are perfections which contain no imperfection in their idea and definition. These, e.g. wisdom, may be found in a finite and otherwise imperfect state in this world, but they need not of their very nature be finite and imperfect. Examples of pure perfections are: intellect, will, goodness, holiness. Other perfections are not pure perfections. In their very idea and definition they contain some inherent imperfection; and these we cannot attribute to God. Such mixed perfections are, for example, materiality, discursive thought, temporal existence, extension—even though it were infinite extension.

These examples and definitions raise still further questions of their own.

(ii) It will be concluded that in God *all pure perfections are united in one absolutely simple perfection.* This conclusion, too, raises, I hope, its own difficulties.

It will be sufficient here to treat the second question in detail; the first can be dealt with piecemeal in treating the separate attributes of God.

The attributes may for convenience be reduced to a short list of two, because all that is required here is to illustrate a principle. Let the two be intellect and will. If the fact of creation be granted, all God's attributes can be shown to be special aspects of these two. I have said that even if we reduce them to one—infinite intellect—a full analysis of this would reveal all the rest. But it will be more helpful to start with two and show how, though in our minds they are distinct and have distinct definitions, yet in God they may very well be identical.

In order to present the problem as forcibly as possible, I begin by observing that the attributes of God, in the way we conceive them, are not synonymous. This is clear because the definition of intellect is not the same as the definition of will; and also because the ideas of intellect and will, as we form them, are not obtained from God but from observing finite creatures in whom intellect and will are not identical. But they must be identical in God, because each is identical with one simple, infinite perfection.

The question is, how can they be? How can infinite intellect and infinite will coincide without both intellect and will losing their identity? Or again: it is said that pure perfections are in God: but does it not seem that we cannot understand what a pure perfection is, since we can only conceive perfections which are distinct from one another, and therefore not infinite?

The clue in the present case is a remarkable one. It consists in showing that there is a closely parallel case in the finite sphere. It can be seen that it is not a phenomenon which is verified in things because they are *finite*, but because

they *are*. It is inseparable from the notion of being as such.
It must therefore be verified pre-eminently in the infinite
source of all finite being.

There are certain notions called the *transcendentals*. Let no
one be put off by a word of many applications. Here it means
something very simple, namely, that the notion of *being*, that
is, of something existent, contains when analysed—or better,
is found when analysed to be identical with—the notions of
unity, truth, and goodness; and some would add beauty to
the list. These notions are called transcendentals because
they run through all possible categories of being and are not
confined to some particular category, as intellect is or red-
ness or finiteness.

Every being, because it is, is *ipso facto*, and in its own
measure, one, and true, and good; and these notions are
mutually inclusive; their partial distinction is the work of the
human mind looking at being from different points of view.

Every being is *one*; and the greater the perfection of the
thing, the greater the essential unity. Unity may be described or detected in various ways: as distinction from other
things—a great man is unique, a dress an exclusive model:
or as resistance to essential division; or as presence to self.
The higher the type of being, the greater the essential unity.
This notion will be further illustrated in dealing with the
simplicity of God. Meanwhile the reader may care to verify
it for himself in stones, plants, animals, man; in works of art
of all kinds; in pure spirit; and finally in God.

Every being is *true*. Truth is the quality of corresponding
with mind; and therefore to say that every being is true is to
say that every being is intelligible. The higher the type of
being, the higher the essential intelligibility and—a point
worth pondering—the greater the effort of *our* mind needed
to understand it. What is very intelligible to us may have

small intelligibility in itself. What is difficult for us to understand may be unintelligible nonsense; but it is best not to
assume too easily that it is.

Every being is, in its degree, *good*. The goodness of a
thing is fundamentally the thing itself regarded as the object
of its own tendency to preserve its own nature as far as it can,
and, by activity, to impart something of its own nature to
other things as far as it can.

Thus the unity, truth and goodness of a thing are found
to be identical, in the thing, with what the thing *is*. The
distinction of the notions is purely the work of our minds
which, having but imperfect insight into existent reality,
must look at it from a number of different points of view. It
is hardly necessary to spend much time applying this principle to the divine attributes. The unity of being is parallel
to the divine unity and simplicity; the truth of being to the
divine intellect; and the goodness of being to the divine will
and goodness. All other positive attributes—wisdom, holiness, justice and the rest—are only further and richer analyses of intellect and will. In man, intellect and will are distinct because by his freedom he is given scope for producing
his own unity; it is not entirely imposed upon him. Even in
man the distinction of intellect and will cannot be in all respects complete. An act of intellect is a self-expression, and
an act of will is informed by intellect. They are distinct
faculties because the human intellect is able to distinguish
different points of view, and also because, among finite objects, a thing may be good as a piece of reality, but not good
for me to choose. For God, intellect and will are one and infinitely good. Even in man, within limits imposed by finiteness, so far as intellect and will are disunited, or able to be
disunited, it argues a want of perfection or of power, or a
moral fault. A man can know God and yet not love Him as

much as he knows Him; he can know what he cannot do; and he can choose what he knows he should not choose. Thus the clue is a double one: there is the horizontal aspect, so to call it, of the transcendentals which run through all being simply because it is being; and there is the vertical aspect, the method of approach or direction-finding, by which greater unity between intellect and will is observed in proportion as perfection of being increases.

As a rider on the principle given above, the following difficulty may be considered. It is sometimes said that finite possibility depends on the divine essence, finite actuality on the divine will, and not *vice versa*. But if God's essence and will are absolutely identical, what is one to make of the distinction? If it means, 'God could not make 2 plus 2 equal to 5, even if He wanted to', this may easily be shown to have no meaning; because 2 plus 2 equals 5 is inherently contradictory, and therefore not something, and therefore not something depending on the divine essence nor a possible object of the divine will. If it means that the fact that a camel is possible depends on the divine essence, and the fact that a camel is actual depends on the divine will and not *vice versa*, it may be replied that the distinction is a human one. The divine freedom to which is attributed the fact of creation is identical with God's essence-will, and its exercise makes no intrinsic difference to God. Whether God creates or does not, He is, and is willing, the same infinite object. How this may be is considered in treating of the divine freedom.

4. *The simplicity of God*

The absolute simplicity of God means that there is in Him no composition of really distinct elements such as matter and form, potency and act, essence and existence, or the parts of a material thing. There is not in Him even the basis for us to form about Him separate thoughts one of which should totally exclude the other. The distinction of the divine attributes, the work of our minds, may be said to be grounded in God in the sense that His one, simple, infinite perfection is by identity intellect, will, goodness, power, and all the rest. These pure perfections He is, not metaphorically but in very truth. And in Him they are all one simple perfection.

The simplicity of God follows from His infinity, or better, His infinity, when further considered, is found to mean His simplicity.

We can say if we wish that man is an animal while excluding from consideration the fact that he is also rational; we can think of man's rationality while excluding from consideration the fact that he is also an animal. There is in man objective ground for this possibility of thought; he is not an animal by virtue of being rational, nor rational in virtue of being an animal. But there cannot be in God objective ground for any such distinction of thoughts about Him. If one thought about Him could adequately exclude another in that way, then at least one of the thoughts would not have an infinite object. Because God is infinite, there can be in Him neither real distinction of elements, nor ground for us to make an adequate distinction of thoughts about Him.

In finite things, simplicity presents something of a paradox. We think of a stone as a simpler thing than a man. But if simplicity is internal unity, and the greater the perfection the greater the unity, then man must have greater essential simplicity than a stone, in spite of his accidental complexity. The greater the essential unity, the greater its power to unify many accidentally diverse elements. A useful test of essential simplicity is resistance to division. To give one example: stone *as such* does not much resist division, in so far as even if it is divided it still remains stone. Some plants and lower animals can be divided without their natures being destroyed. Man's body can be divided without being destroyed, only to a limited degree. Spirit as such cannot be divided; there is no point of insertion, so to speak, for division. The same test can be applied to works of art of all descriptions. One may compare a block of flats with Westminster Abbey from this point of view; or one may compare bagpipe music with Brahms's Fourth Symphony.

It is a rather sobering thought that we learn from revelation that absolute simplicity is, in fact, threeness of Persons in unity of nature. St Thomas, with disarming blandness, points out that the threeness of Persons does not interfere with the unity of nature, since the nature is one, not three, and the Persons are compared as distinct, not as parts of a whole. Needless to say, his intention was not to explain the mystery of the Blessed Trinity.[1]

One consequence of the absolute simplicity of God is that since God is not compounded of substance and accidents, there can be no real relation of God towards the world; in other words, the fact that God is creator and conserver of the world and knows the world, makes absolutely no real difference in God. Put in human language, these facts sound astonishing, impossible, and even shocking. But this is technical language whose bearing can only be appreciated by study and slow acclimatization. Here it needs to be offset by the certain fact that God is in very truth creator, conserver and lover of the world. The world is indeed included in the object of His infinite love.

We cannot see directly how this conclusion, that creation does not set up a real relation of God to the world, is verified in God. But gradually one can acquire, not insight, but a

[1] *De Potentia Dei*, 7:1, reply to objection 10.

presage of insight. One can overcome the tendency to think of God as a being among beings, subject to the inevitable relations and dependencies of finite things among themselves. It can gradually come to mean more that God's transcendence is no mere refuge of our ignorance, but infinite intelligibility, inviting us and, in a measure, enabling us, even in this life, to know Him as He wishes to be known.

5. *The unicity of God*

'There is only one God', says the Catechism, and it is hardly necessary today to spend much time in showing that if God exists He must also be one.

Unicity, or uniqueness, is part of the ultimate perfection of unity, and therefore it must be attributed to the nature of God. If there were more than one God, each would not have perfect unity, for each would be compounded of nature and individuality; that by which each was God would not be the same as that by which each was *this* God.

The unicity of God has its reflection in this world; not indeed in natures, for if, following St Thomas, we except the specific natures of the angels, we know of no nature that might not be multiplied. But the individual *as such* cannot be multiplied: each individual man is necessarily unique.

It might seem a drawback that God should be unique. Would it not be an added perfection, an added happiness, for God to know and love His like? In philosophy one might reply with perfect justice that the infinite is utterly self-sufficient and needs no other to consort with. This would be a true and good reason. Yet the revealed doctrine of three Persons in one God, of family life as a divine and not merely a human thing, cannot but seem right and comforting to minds made for God.

6. *The eternity of God*

The eternity of God is a particularly helpful attribute to reflect on, because it seems to present both the question, 'What
sort of knowledge have we of God?' and its answer, in a
specially clear light. 'The eternity of God escapes us
absolutely', says the *Dictionnaire de Théologie Catholique*, meaning thereby that we have absolutely no *direct* grasp of
eternity, but not that we are in a state of total ignorance
about it. Eternity can be defined clearly, in terms that give
analogical knowledge of it.

Eternity is the existence of God in its condition of being
without beginning and end, and *without succession*.

Undoubtedly people all begin trying to understand
eternity by means of the frontal attack: eternity is thought
of as never-ending time. But it has been well said that
never-ending time is almost the opposite of eternity, because
never-ending time is never-ending succession, and God's
eternity excludes all succession.

The word eternity is also used in a less strict sense to
mean duration without beginning, or without end, or without both. An eternal world would mean a world that had
no beginning. In the same way the human soul may be
called eternal in so far as it will have no end. But both an
eternal world and eternal souls are subject to succession,
whereas God's eternity excludes succession.

Time has been described as *nunc fluens*, a flowing 'now';
the duration of angels as *nunc saltans*, a series of discontinu-
ous 'nows'—their acts of intellect and will are a series, but
each act is without internal succession; God's eternity as
nunc stans, a static 'now'.

The definition of eternity given by Boethius (d. 522) has
become famous, and is used by St Thomas: God's eternity
is *interminabilis vitae tota simul et perfecta possessio*—life without

limits, possessed perfectly and as a simultaneous whole. The essentials of this definition are two: *interminabilis*, which excludes beginning and end and their possibility; and *tota simul*, which excludes succession and its possibility. The remaining elements of the definition are merely explicative: *life*, because God's eternity is in fact eternity of life; *possession*, rather than duration, because possession conveys the idea of stability and rest better than the word duration, which rather suggests succession; *perfect* possession, because the simultaneity of eternity is not that of a point of time, the slenderest of realities, but of its opposite, the possession of infinite being.

God must be eternal. He is the one being whose nature is existence: thus are excluded from Him beginning and end, for essential existence cannot not-exist. He is infinite existence: thus is excluded from Him the possibility of succession. For if there were in God any succession, He would proceed from being to different being, and would not be of His nature infinite Being.

An ancient controversy whether God and temporal things can be said to co-exist seems to present an unreal problem. To co-exist is to have a common 'now'; but the 'now' of time and the 'now' of eternity have nothing in common to provide a basis for direct comparison.

Philosophers and poets have in all ages felt and tried to express clues or presages of insight into eternity. In contemporary poetry one may recall Mr T. S. Eliot's *Four Quartets*. Philosophers have suggested the man on top of a mountain who sees at a glance what the men below must make their way round to see; or the man on a tower seeing the whole long column filing by, while each member of the column sees only a part of it. Or again, eternity has been compared with the still point of a circle, time with the tracing of the circumference. Or one might reverse the last example and think of eternity as an immense circle and time as a short line within it. But all these clues, suggestive as they are, valuable as they are, only serve to bring home more clearly that we have no direct insight.

Love, and the love of things called art, can create the impression that time stands still; or that we can leap over time, span it all from a new height. All great artists are able on occasion and in their various ways, to do this for us. Even in the everyday working of the mind, through memory and imagination, we can in a measure transcend succession. Every intellectual concept is timeless in a sense—in the sense that it does not itself include time, that it abstracts from time. Such abstraction produces what is called 'negative eternity'. This is not God's eternity, not totally free from every kind of succession, because it is not God's infinity. Yet to the mind in some moods it is so suggestive that some have made the mistake of concluding that intellectual concepts give direct insight into the mind of God.

7. *The immensity and ubiquity of God*

The immensity of God is the divine Being in so far as it is able to be, and must necessarily be, present as creative agent to every possible creature, immediately, and without change in Himself. The ubiquity of God is the divine Being in so far as it is in fact present to actual creatures.

This presence of God is simply and solely our way of expressing His immediate agency as creator and conserver of the world. God's creatures include things which are spatial and local: His creative presence, which is Himself, is thereby spatial and local in no way whatever. If it be thought that the very word 'presence' includes a local or spatial connotation in the thing that is present, then God's presence to things is not literal but metaphorical only; if on the other hand it be allowed that the word 'presence' can be used to mean any immediacy, and in particular the immediate causality exercised by God, then God's presence is not merely metaphorical, but literal.

St Thomas points out that God's presence may be thought of as presence by His *power*, in so far as all creation must be immediately subject to His power; by His *knowledge*, in so far as He knows all creation with perfect knowledge; and by His *essence*, in so far as His essence is the creative agent and is not distinct from His power. These different aspects of God's presence can be distinguished if it is found helpful; but it has to be remembered that in God essence, power, knowledge, agency, are all absolutely one.

This, in philosophy, is the way in which 'God is everywhere'. In Holy Scripture God is represented to mankind largely in the language of metaphor. The moral would seem to be that philosophic apprehension is only a part, and perhaps not the most necessary part, of human apprehension.

In the early eighteenth century Newton and some of his followers held a theory that confused God's immensity with imaginary, unlimited space which, by a further error, they held to have actual existence independently of spatial things.

Once it is clearly apprehended that God Himself is in no way spatial or local, the question whether He might not be operative at a distance is seen to have no meaning.

What is the meaning, in this context, of *immediate* presence? It means that God's creative agency is without intermediary, but in a special sense. As will be shown in due place, God does use creatures as instruments of His causality, but He is present to the instrument, in and through the instrument, in such a way that the causality of the instrument does not exclude His own immediate causality; somewhat as the appearance of a river depends both on the river and on the light that shines through it. In such cases God and His instruments are both immediate causes, but in different orders. When it is said that God is present to things, in things, through things, the meaning is that every part of a thing is equally in need of God's causal presence.

Perhaps the most obvious question suggested by God's presence is that of His immutability. God does not change by being immediately present as creative cause.

8. *The immutability of God*

The immutability of God means just what it seems to mean: that there is not and cannot be in God any kind of change whatever. God as creator is exactly the same as He would have been if He had freely chosen not to create. We have, as always, no direct insight into this conclusion, and we have perhaps less clues than usual. It can hardly be pointed out too often that when once a certain truth about God has been established, the difficulties which remain can in principle be neglected as irrelevant; they are all of human manufacture; God Himself is not difficult, but supreme intelligibility. Yet if we want, as we should, to have our self-made difficulties relieved as far as possible, the habit of reflection on the infinite can suggest formulae which to some extent can mitigate the effects of our finite-mindedness. Infinite will, we may reflect, needs and can have nothing additional in order freely to will and effect the finite. The perfect act includes the imperfect. God's act of will is perfect, and transcends the finite acts of will which in ourselves would be necessary to produce freely in ourselves or outside ourselves voluntary finite effects. It is an imperfection of freedom to have to change oneself first in order to produce a finite effect. Yet even a man can produce effects on others without changing. Infinite freedom is freedom to will an infinite object without impediment interior or exterior. The necessity of changing oneself first would be an imperfection and to that extent an impediment. An infinite will already possesses all it can choose to possess or to will, because the finite adds nothing to the infinite. Whether these considerations seem to have much force or not—and by quiet reflection they can come to have considerable force—we can once more affirm that to expect or attempt to find a complete solution of this and similar problems would be a mistake of method. Such problems must always remain. There must always be an insoluble residue; because the only complete solution would be to have direct insight into the essence of God, and this we cannot have.

The search for clues is an attempt to exclude as far as possible human errors and misunderstandings, one of which may be mentioned here. The difference between creation and finite causality is considerable, but one thing they have in common: an agent as such, whether finite or infinite, does not change in acting. An agent does not move in so far as it acts, but only in so far as it is acted upon. Any agent, even a finite agent, acts simply by being. Whether it produces an effect or not depends, in the case of a finite agent, on whether there is anything within its sphere of influence. The principle often causes great surprise on first hearing. I knock my hand against a table and it bruises me; the table does not move in doing so. The slight movement of the table is due to my action on it, not its action on me. I move my hand up to the table to give and receive an effect. The movement as such of my hand is not an acting but a being-acted-upon—in this case by my will through my muscles. In willing to move my hand I change my will, because as man I have the power to do so. This power is given me by God, and through secondary causes is supplied with all the prerequisites for willing. But precisely as agent my human nature does not change; it changes only in so far as it is acted upon by myself *qua* agent or by some other. Nor does God change in creating and conserving me. The difficulty remains that we imagine God must change His will in order to produce external effects. But that is wholly the work of our minds. We say God is infinite, and then proceed to think of Him as finite.

The paradoxical facts may now be repeated in all their starkness. Infinite necessity and infinite freedom are identical in God; the height of freedom is to will infinite good without hindrance interior or exterior; the free will to create finite things makes no difference whatever to a will whose object is infinite good.

On these principles rests ultimately the answer to certain more popular difficulties. If God is unchangeable, what use is it to pray? The sufficient immediate answer is that the prayers and the answer to them are part of the order of creation known and willed in God's eternity. Again, in Holy Scripture God is said to turn from displeasure to love towards the converted sinner. Displeasure as a variable condition is of course attributed to God by a metaphor. Yet even human love is compatible with displeasure. Infinite love, while it cannot have displeasure as a subjective and variable condition, can produce the effects of displeasure; the effect of infinite love on free creatures varies according to their different dispositions, as the same sun melts wax and hardens mud.

5

God's Knowledge

1. *God's infinite intellect*

GOD is infinite intellect in which knower and known are identical. The distinction we draw between knower and known is transcended in God. The suspicion, drawn out into a thesis and strongly insisted on by some philosophers, that thought and object of thought must always be distinct, is one more product of our experience of finite thought; it is a duality that finite thought can never wholly transcend.

At the same time there is room for caution in conclusions about the nature of the absolute simplicity of infinite intellect; for we learn from revelation that it is constituted by threeness of Persons; and in theology the Second Person is described as the Word or thought of the First Person—a really distinct Person, yet identical in Godhead. Philosophy could not suspect the truth in this form, and theology can state it, but does not profess to explain it. The parallel may here be noted between supernatural mysteries and purely philosophical conclusions about God, which always contain an element of natural mystery, that is, mystery whose terms we can discover for ourselves but cannot positively reconcile. The object of such mysteries, natural and supernatural, is supreme intelligibility which the finite mind is not big enough to grasp. But the terms of the mysteries are in all cases intelligible; and they never announce an open contradiction. If, for instance, the mystery of the Blessed Trinity declared that Three Persons were One Person, no one could accept it.

When it is said that God is intellect, what is meant by intellect? It means that, though we have no direct insight into the divine intellect, we can know this much about it, that it does not exclude the essential of intellect as we understand it, namely, awareness, consciousness, grasp of the intelligible. How is it known that the infinite, transcending the finite, does not thereby *exclude* what to our minds is the essential perfection of intellect? Only indirectly. If infinite existence excluded this essential perfection of awareness conscious grasp of the intelligible, then God would be no infinite perfection, but less than human. Knowing neither Himself nor the world, He would be as much a mere passive object of human speculation and curiosity as the material world is. Is there any essentially more direct way of showing that infinite perfection is *ipso facto* conscious intellect, or better, that infinite intellect is not a contradiction? It does not seem so. One may use the approach of ascending perfection, and point out that the higher the being the higher the unity; and that to know oneself is greater presence to self than not to know oneself. But this does not seem to amount to more than the indirect showing given above.

Plotinus, expressing the transcendence of God in an exaggerated way, held that God is not conscious but beyond consciousness; though whether by that he meant to say that God is simply not conscious may be doubted. Yet there is a tendency for some minds, or for the mind in some moods, to rest in the thought of an unconscious, impersonal ultimate reality. Possibly the imperfect sources from which

we first acquire our notions of personality have something to do with it. Things reflect God perfectly, each in its
own degree; only men do not. One can sympathize with
those who prefer God's workshop to man's. According to
Aristotle, God is conscious of Himself but not of the world.
Thus in the behaviour of the world we should have the effects
of intellect without intellect. The Stoics made God a sort of
soul of the world, attributing to Him loving providence,
and directing to Him a piety at times almost Christian in
tone. That the Stoics mistakenly declared everything,
God included, to be material, is perhaps not specially
significant in this connection; that may well be rather a
matter of words. More significant is the fact that for them
there is something impersonal about God's providence. It is
benevolent but fatalistic; all we can do is to accept it, con-
form ourselves with it. In a fuller context and with different
emphasis, even that might be given an acceptable interpretation. But for the Stoics, individual personal relations
between God and man were minimized at best. Again, the
modern scientific mind often professes to find little or no
difficulty in accepting the effects of intellect without intellect
itself; to accept as ultimate reality a purely material
universe, whose nature it should be to evolve into an ordered
complexity, throwing up on to the shores of the world life
which should here and there develop into mind. To them
the Hebrew attitude to God as expressed, for example, in
the Psalms, would seem radically anthropomorphic, not
merely in accepting a personal God at all, but still more in
its highly personal attitude to His providence, not to mention the Hebrew sense of sin. The truth seems to be that it
takes sustained intellectual courage to be able to square
one's shoulders and face the thought of God as at once *my*
God and infinite, unchanging spirit. Plato in intention came

not far from it; but few, it seems, would have shared his human hope, now buoyantly confident, now mournful, save for the revelation he never consciously knew yet felt the need of, and the Incarnation.

2. *The objects of God's knowledge*

God, by His infinite act of knowledge, knows Himself in every way in which He is knowable. It can be concluded that this infinite act includes knowledge of the power to create this world and other possible worlds, in every way in which actual and possible worlds are knowable, that is, not only in a general way, but in complete detail.

If we had nothing to go on except our idea of infinite knowledge, we might have concluded with Aristotle that divine knowledge does not include the knowledge of finite things, and the power to create them. We have to look elsewhere for guidance. In due place the following conclusions will be drawn, each for its own reasons, and independently of the present question: that God created the world; that He conserves it directly, and co-operates with it immediately in all its activities, and directs the whole of creation to the end for which He created it; that creation is a free choice of God and not a necessary act—free not only with respect to creating or not creating, but also to creating this world or some other possible world. These conclusions imply in turn what it is the immediate concern here to show, namely, that God knows this world and all possible worlds in complete detail.

God's knowledge is all derived from Himself, never from any other source. This is evident from the consideration that God must be utterly independent of creation which, on the other hand, must be utterly dependent on Him. God's knowledge is God's being, and His being is by definition *a se*, underived, its own explanation in every way. In knowing Himself, God knows all possibilities and all actuality, because these both depend directly on Him. The fact that acts of our free will depend directly on God as well as directly on ourselves will be explained in due place.

One question which arises from the divine knowledge of finite possibility is: If God knows all this detail, what becomes of His absolute simplicity? Here the briefest answer is the best: We cannot see directly, but we have the clue that finite objects of knowledge add nothing to an infinite act of knowledge, but must be held to be part of its definition. This is a clue only, and not insight; the difficulty arises because we tend to think of God as finite. The doctrine of divine ideas has a long and in some ways a distinguished history. St Augustine adapted it to his own use from Plato; the pseudo-Denys makes much of it; medieval theology is full of it; St Thomas, with his strong respect for tradition, explains it at length; a modern Thomist calls the doctrine 'a useless fiction'.[1] This startling difference of emphasis is due to circumstances of history, and need not detain us. All it is necessary to say is that God's one, simple act of knowledge includes the knowledge of all finite possibility and actuality.

3. *God's knowledge of free acts*

God's knowledge of *actual* free acts presents no initial difficulty in the light of the doctrine of eternity. By His eternal knowledge God simply knows: there is in His knowledge no temporal distinction of past, present and future. This may seem a straightforward conclusion, and so it is;

[1] E. de Bruyne, *S. Thomas d'Aquin*, p. 158.

but there is more in it than meets the eye. At first we think of God's eternal knowledge of the world as like a picture seen all at once, and that is not a bad image as far as it goes. But we are brought up sharp when we remember that God's knowledge is not derived from the world, is not dependent on the world, but on the contrary the world depends on God's knowledge, that is, on God. If the question is asked, how does God's knowledge of free acts not interfere with human freedom? it can be answered that just as our knowledge of our own and other people's present and past free acts does not interfere with their freedom, so God's eternal knowledge of our free acts, past, present and future, does not interfere with their freedom: that to eternal knowledge, temporal future is just as present as temporal present and past; and that God's knowledge is not foreknowledge, though it is sometimes so called for convenience. All this again is perfectly true as far as it goes, but it does not go to the heart of the difficulty, which is that God's knowledge is absolutely independent of what happens in the world, and therefore, while it is not foreknowledge in a temporal sense, it has a priority-by-nature, a priority-by-independence. To confine the matter to the sphere of free choice, the only sphere where God's knowledge presents very notable difficulty, free actions happen because God wills the good actions to take place, and wills to allow the bad actions to take their course. The questions arise: (i) What is the correlation between God's willing men's good free actions to take place, and their happening? If God positively wills them to take place —as He does—does this not interfere with human freedom? (ii) What is the correlation between God's willing to allow bad actions to take their course, and the actual occurrence of bad actions?

To the first of these questions, after eliminating misunderstandings, a very satisfactory answer can be given. To the second question a sufficient answer can be given, but one that is more remote from the finite understanding. The best that can be done is to present the situation as objectively as possible, and to try to let the facts speak for themselves so far as human thought and language will allow.

One very important point may be cleared up from the start, namely, that once it is realized that God's eternal knowledge does not in any way depend on the world, *the difficulty about hypothetical free acts is neither greater nor less than the difficulty about His knowledge of actual free acts*. By hypothetical free acts we mean what a man—real or imaginary—would do in circumstances which do not, in fact, arise. This definition has about it an uncomfortable air of unreality. Nevertheless, as will be seen in the event, it is sufficient for our purpose. At first the difficulty of hypothetical free acts seems more formidable, but it is not. The problem is clear enough: freedom in this world is normally freedom to choose between alternatives, call them X and not-X; and only the man's actual choice can settle our doubt about which he will choose. Christ in the Gospel declares what Tyre and Sidon would have done if He had worked miracles among them. Did He mean that He was absolutely certain? And if so, how could He be? Now, this problem is not essentially different from that of His knowledge of actual free acts. The priority-by-nature or priority-by-independence of the divine knowledge makes this evident.

It has been thought a remarkable fact that St Thomas, while he has much to say about God's knowledge of actual free acts, has no separate treatment of His knowledge of hypothetical free acts. But since the two questions are essentially the same, no separate theory was required. This, however, makes it all the more necessary to determine what

St Thomas really says and means about actual free acts, and to this we now proceed.[1]

St Thomas holds: (i) God knows all actual things, past, present and future; and also all possible but not actual things. God's knowledge, in so far as it covers actual things, is called *scientia visionis*, the knowledge of vision; in so far as it covers things possible but not actual, it is called *scientia simplicis intelligentiae*, the knowledge of mere understanding. About God's knowledge of hypothetical free acts St Thomas has nothing special to say.

(ii) Actual *good* actions take place because God positively wills them to take place as the sort of things they are, i.e., as good actions freely produced by a man. How God can positively will a man's good actions to take place without detriment to their freedom will be considered presently. Actual *bad* actions take place because God wills to allow them to take place as the sort of things they are, i.e., as actions forbidden, but not impeded, by Himself, their badness as such being produced entirely by the creature. The creature alone can produce the badness, because badness as such is a falling away from due perfection, and is not something positive.

The essential difference between the divine will with respect to good actions and with respect to bad actions may be illustrated a little further. In both cases the divine will is operative but, in St Thomas's summary, 'God therefore neither wills bad actions to take place nor wills bad actions not to take place, but wills to allow bad actions to take

---

[1] For the signposting of the relevant writings of St Thomas I am greatly indebted to the masterly articles of Fr Bernard Lonergan, S.J., in *Theological Studies*, Vol. 3 (1942), pp. 375–402, 533–53, in the series under the general title of *St Thomas's Thought on Gratia Operans*. For the details of interpretation and application, while here again I owe much to Fr Lonergan, the responsibility must be my own.

place; and to do so is good.'[1] Similarly in a theological context St Thomas draws out the difference between predestination and reprobation: predestination is the *cause* of grace and of glory; but reprobation is not the cause of the sin that leads to the loss of God, but 'sin comes from the free will of the person who suffers reprobation.'[2] And, in general, God's allowing of bad actions to take their course is not the cause of their happening, either positively, by forcing the action, or negatively, by unjustly withholding from the man the power necessary to produce a good action.[3]

(iii) How does God infallibly know and efficaciously will men's good actions without detriment to their freedom? The answer is, because of the *transcendence* of the divine intellect and will. And this reason is no mere refuge of our ignorance, but, when properly understood, a truly sufficient explanation. I paraphrase St Thomas, *Peri Hermeneias*, I:14:22:

> The divine will is to be understood as existing outside the order of finite things. It must be envisaged as a cause from which proceeds the whole of finite being in all its diverse kinds. Now, finite being may be divided into the free and the necessary (or not-free); and so we say that actions both free and not free have their origin in the divine will; and the same applies to the different proximate causes required to produce these two types of action. Where God wishes non-free actions to be produced, he provides non-free agents; where He wishes free actions to be produced, He provides free agents, that is, agents which can fail (and thereby produce morally bad actions). Thus, according as the agents are free or not free, we call the actions free or

[1] *Deus igitur neque vult mala fieri, neque vult mala non fieri, sed vult permittere mala fieri, et hoc est bonum. Summa Theologica*, I:19:9, reply to objection 3.
[2] *Summa Theologica*, I:23:3, reply to objection 2.
[3] cf. *Summa Theologica*, I:49:1–3; I-2:79:1–3; *De Malo*, 3:1–2.

not free; but for all their difference, they all depend equally on the divine will as on the First Cause which *transcends* the difference of free and not-free. And this transcending of free and not-free is not something that can be said of the human will, nor of any other cause, but only of the divine will.

Contra Gentiles, 3:94:

> The work of divine providence, therefore, includes not merely the production of this or that effect, but the production of some effects as free and others as not free. Some of the actions which are subject to divine providence are free; they are not all determined . . . thus (our actions) are 'foreseen' (so to speak) by God as actions which are produced freely by ourselves.

Summa Theologica, 1:19:8 (*Whether the divine will imposes necessity on things*):

> Since, then, the divine will is able to produce every possible type of being without difficulty or restriction, it follows not merely that whatever God wants to take place does take place, but also that it takes place in the way God wants it to take place. And He wants some things to take place as determined (i.e. not free), and other things to take place as free, in order to produce in the universe a full complement of the different types of being. . . .

Now to search for clues. The essential clue in the present matter may be found by thinking about human liberty. Briefly, if we think out human liberty properly, we ought to conclude that God's causing of our good free acts is *in itself* more intelligible than God's causing a stone to act like a stone. But at first it does not seem so to us. Let us try to see why.

For us, the typical cause, that by comparison with which other sorts of cause are understood, is the material, determined cause. For God, the typical cause is His own infinite

Being. Between these two, and of incomparably greater perfection than the first, though still of incomparably less perfection than the second, is the free human cause. In fact, a good human action is, naturally speaking, beyond all comparison the highest example of created good in this world. The essence of free human causality is self-determination; its essential good is self-determination in good. The greater the degree of self-determination in good, the greater the perfection of any being. By self-determination in good we participate in God's self-determination in good. Our freedom is a participation in God's freedom. Our freedom, as a thing of incomparably greater perfection than determined, non-free being, is in itself of incomparably greater intelligibility. But this essentially greater intelligibility of human freedom would not belong to it if the difficulty of understanding how God can give self-determination were essential to the notion of freedom, and not accidental. We tend to think that God cannot *give* human freedom and its exercise, cannot *give self*-determination in good without thereby destroying it: so little insight have we into the nature of freedom, so much less into the nature of God; so bound are our minds, in their direct insight, not merely to the finite but even to the material.

(iv) The next relevant fact is that the infallibility of the divine knowledge is always explained by St Thomas by reference to the divine eternity and immutability: for God all is present. His knowledge of free human acts, good or bad, is infallible with what is called *necessitas ex suppositione*, or hypothetical necessity, as frequently illustrated by St Thomas by the example *Socrates dum sedet non potest non sedere*: while he is sitting down, Socrates cannot be not sitting down. This, so far as it goes, meets the difficulty that God's infallible knowledge or will seems to interfere with human freedom. Just as our certain knowledge of our own and other people's past and present free acts does not interfere with their freedom, so neither does God's eternal knowledge of our free acts, past, present and future, interfere with their freedom. This is a perfectly good answer as far as it goes, and in fact St Thomas does not go further. But a further question lurks behind this reply. So far as good actions are concerned, no difficulty remains after the explanation given in (iii) above. But what is the nature of the correlation between God's permission of evil and man's commission of it? Knowledge of evil committed is part of God's eternal knowledge of the world; *but His eternal knowledge is not obtained from creatures.* God knows these things because He wills and causes them. But what can be said about His will in so far as it is the will to allow evil?

(v) Another way of putting what was said about bad actions in (ii) above would be to say that sin, in its own nature, is *absolutely unintelligible.* That is, it has no positive being, and no positive cause, human or divine. Its cause is not efficient, but deficient—the deficient human will. It has no connection with being or with truth except as a deprivation of both. It is inexplicable except as a brute fact freely produced by the creature. This needs a little more elucidation, but first I will paraphrase another short passage from St Thomas, *Summa Theologica,* 1:17:1:

> In things which depend on God, falsehood, that is, want of correspondence with the divine intellect, can never be found; because everything that happens in the world is planned by the divine mind. The only possible exception is that found in free creatures, who have the power to withdraw themselves from the order planned by the divine intellect. That is what sin involves; and that is the sense in which sins are called 'falsehoods' and 'lies' in Holy Scripture.

Nevertheless, God knows the fact of evil, and His plan for the world is not spoiled by it. This plan, as taking account of the fact of sin, may be described as the will to create a world in which evil is allowed to take its course; and this, says St Thomas, is a good plan, entirely worthy of the divine will.

It might seem strange to say that sin is 'absolutely unintelligible'. If we ask ourselves why we committed a sin, we can usually give some sort of reason. Further, the possibility of sin is intelligible in so far as it is clear that for free creatures who have only an imperfect, though sufficient, grasp of the good they ought to choose, failure is always a possibility. But what is meant is, first, that sin is always irrational. It depends on a self-deception by which a man says, 'This is good for me as a man', when he knows it is not. And if one looks for the reason why the irrational happened, one cannot look further than the fact that the man freely allowed it to happen. Extenuations of all kinds there may be and often are; but in so far as it was voluntary and avoidable, a man can blame none but himself, and certainly not God. Thus with St Thomas we answer the questions: 'What is sin? What relation has it to the human will? To the divine will?'

There St Thomas leaves the whole matter, and there, too, we can profitably leave it if we wish. There has been no notable advance in the understanding of the question since St Thomas wrote, and there have been several notable retrogressions which may serve as salutary warnings to the venturesome. All that can be done is to offer points of view with due diffidence and caution. One such is as follows. There is a sense in which possibility includes not only what God can will-to-produce, but also what He can will-to-permit. God can know both these possibilities, because, in fact, He knows such examples of them as exist in this world. The general situation might then be formulated thus: God knows everything possible *as the sort of thing it is*. He knows what He can will-to-produce as the sort of thing it is, namely, as good which He positively wills and the creature freely produces. He knows what He can will-to-permit as the sort of thing it is, namely, as forbidden by Himself, but induced freely and deficiently by the creature only, and allowed to take its course. When God chooses to create a possible world, He can choose any world that does not contradict His nature, His attributes. How far the range of such worlds extends, we cannot be very sure; but we know at least that this world is included in the range, and that in general God can will-to-produce good and will-to-allow evil without prejudice to any of His attributes. God's 'antecedent' view of the world as possible may be reasonably thought of as like our retrospective view of it as actual; that would seem to be an objective way of looking at it. We know things for what they are; God knows things, actual and possible, past present and future, for what they are. On this view it might seem less important to insist strongly, with certain scholastic philosophers and theologians, on the difference between what a man *could* do, say, X and not-X, and what a man *would* do, say, X, and call the first 'possibles', and the second a 'futurible'. A real world is a world in which men do free actions, not a world in which they hang for ever suspended among possibles; and a free action normally involves alternatives *before* the action, but excludes alternatives *in* the action. Here, of course, the problem of God's knowledge touches the problem of evil. God's will-to-permit evil would seem to be the fact about Him least readily available to our understanding. If at this point we search for clues, if we hope for the beginning of real understanding, at least let us set out convinced that here if anywhere is work for those who realize that their first duty to God is to love and adore Him.

For completeness a word should be added about the history of this famous question. Early Christian writers who touch on the point of God's knowledge of hypothetical free acts assume from Holy Scripture and from the infinity of the divine knowledge that God does have knowledge of such possibilities. St Augustine in wrestling with the problem of evil and human freedom does the same, and upholds both the independence of God and the fact of human freedom. St Thomas's teaching is what has been said. After about the year 1580, theological controversy became acute and theories multiplied, of which the following are samples: 1. That God knows hypothetical free acts by His perfect knowledge of the agent concerned and the circumstances in which he is conceived as placed. This is an impossible theory because it destroys human liberty by making a man's free actions wholly dependent on his antecedents and his circumstances. 2. That God knows such hypothetical free acts by knowing what 'physical predetermination' He would give to such a man in such circumstances. This theory amply safeguards the independence of God, but is open to two objections: (*a*) it assigns to a created entity, namely the physical predetermination itself, conceived as something produced by God in the agent before the action, a transcendence in causality which belongs to God alone. Transfer this imaginary entity to God, and good free actions are readily explained, but bad free actions remain to be explained; (*b*) the theory analyses causality in such a way as to say that an agent requires something additional in order to be active. This seems to be a mistake. Each type of agent needs the internal equipment and the external circumstances needed for each type of action, but for the action itself no additional actuation is required. The agent is agent simply by being what it is. 3. The theory of *scientia media*, or intermediate knowledge—a special kind of knowledge not reducible either to wholly necessary knowledge or to wholly contingent knowledge—whereby God knows such hypothetical free acts. Stripped of inessentials the theory states: that God has such knowledge; that the knowledge is independent of creatures and does not interfere with human freedom; and that we cannot explain the matter any further.

It seems specially in point here to repeat what has been said before, that controversy on this and similar questions seems to have produced over the centuries an unconscious but deeply ingrained and serious mistake of method. It has come to be taken for granted that in principle we ought to be able to explain God; and to be forgotten that we ought to sit lightly to human formulae which, even when free from all positive error, are never univocal in meaning, and always point beyond themselves to God; and that if we forget this basic fact, we can only produce a crop of artificial problems which naturally enough we cannot solve.

6

God's Will and Operation

1. *God's infinite will*

GOD'S infinite will is His infinite being under the aspect of self-expression or self-assertion. All being whatever, by its very being, nature and notion, apart from all idea of movement, is dynamic self-expression or self-assertion. Will in general is this self-assertion as informed by intellect. In God it is identical with intellect.

Will in ourselves can have as its object what we do not possess, and so it can be called desire. Not so in God, who possesses His own infinite being, so that the object of His will cannot be increased. If rest and joy in the possession of the object of will are called love, God is infinite love.

Nevertheless we can speak of primary and secondary objects of the divine will just as we can of the divine intellect. The primary object, that which is willed necessarily and for its own sake is, to make the convenient human distinction, the divine goodness. The secondary objects are all finite possibility and actuality; and these are willed not for their own sakes, not for their own goodness, but because of their connection with, their derivation from, infinite goodnesss. If any finite good were willed by God for its own sake, God would have need of it and would depend on it. Thus the only 'formal object' of the divine will is the divine goodness.

By formal object is meant, again in human but admissible terms, the aspect under which God wills what He wills. This aspect is His own goodness, and finite things are willed and loved because of their connection with His goodness, their dependence on it, their likeness to it.

The phrases used to describe these things are usually employed in speaking of finite being, and when used of God may give rise to misunderstanding. Thus when it is said that God loves the world not for its own sake but for His own sake, the false impression may be given that God's love is selfish. Is it not perfect love, men say, to love another for that person's own sake and not for our own sake?—for that person's good and with no thought of our own good? And so in explaining the unique thing which is God's love it has to be recalled that God cannot possibly get anything out of finite things, and therefore His love of them cannot be selfish in that sense; secondly, that there could not be a better reason for loving things than the fact that they are like God, and that is God's reason for loving them; and finally, when we consider God's love we have to remember to reverse our point of view and stand on our heads. God is and must be the centre of things, and Himself must rightly be the centre of His love; we are not and cannot be the centre of things, and ourselves cannot rightly be the centre of our love. To be self-centred is bad for us because we are not the centre; to be self-centred is good in God because He is the centre. And His being so, makes His love of creatures the love of pure benevolence, and gives to things the value they possess, the dignity of being works of God.

It is very much like a photograph. A photograph is an analogical likeness of a man; a man is an analogical likeness of God. A photograph is valued not because it is a piece of paper with a picture on, but because it is the likeness of a friend. So God loves men because they are likenesses of His goodness; and now in a special sense likenesses of His Son.

To paraphrase St Thomas:

> God loves other things because of their connection with His goodness; but not in such a way as to gain anything from them, as we do when we do good to others, but in such a way as to bestow benefits on them by means of His goodness. And so, as Avicenna says, liberality is a kind of hall-mark of God, because He does not look to any advantage to Himself in His creative activity, but wants His goodness to overflow on to others. In this sense Augustine says that God makes use of us for His own goodness and for our advantage.[1]

God's love of Himself is His being, and is the same necessity. On the other hand, this love or will does not necessarily issue in creation. Creation is a free choice of God. *Bonum est diffusivum sui*, says the neo-Platonic adage: good tends to diffuse itself; and this is true of finite things which are always interactive. But as applied to infinite good, it cannot imply any necessity for creation. God, supremely self-sufficient, can have no necessary reason for producing what is in no way necessary to Himself, in no way increases His perfection and beatitude. That His infinite goodness can be also His sufficient reason for creating, we know from the fact of creation. In the history of philosophy it has seemed to some, even to several Catholic philosophers, a hard saying, that creation is no necessity, physical or moral. One of the most famous names in this connection is that of Leibniz, who held that creation is so in keeping with the nature of God, so becomes God, as to amount to a moral necessity not merely to create, but to create the best of all possible worlds. Perhaps if it were not for revelation we should find it less easy

[1] I Sent, 45:1:2.

to resist such conclusions; and yet the reason that can be given to exclude them is a good and sufficient one, and covers not only the will to create but also the will to choose this world rather than some other possible world. One may speak of other possible world-orders because there is no reason to doubt their possibility. Indeed, finite being by its very notion implies the possibility of more and less. It is well, however, to beware of assuming too much about the range of what is possible and what is not. But as to the 'best of all possible worlds', the idea would seem to be self-contradictory. A particular finite good, by its very finiteness, can always be greater. The sufficient reason for God's choice of this world is the reason He has for all He wills— His own goodness and His own freedom. If we ask ourselves why we choose a particular good, the final and sufficient reason is that the object is (or seems to us) good, and that we freely choose it. The object of God's will is always one and the same—His goodness; that, with the freedom of His will to create, is the only explanation possible or necessary. His one infinite will transcends and explains all the plurality and diversity implied by possible and actual free choice of the finite. Ultimately, diversity cannot be explained by diversity; one must have recourse to unity.

2. *Creation*

God's production of the world must be either by emanation of part of His very substance, or by creation 'out of nothing': it can be shown that it cannot be the former, and it is concluded that it must be the latter. The reasons that can be given are sound ones; but here again, if it were not for relevation, one would not, perhaps, feel so confident about them.

Emanation of the very substance of God is excluded as an explanation of the production of the finite on the ground that this would imply potentiality for division in God, whereas infinite spirit, in virtue of its absolute simplicity, can have no such potentiality. To object that God could lose a portion of Himself without thereby being any the less is to be betrayed by the imagination. The reason given holds: what could be divided from God would be God neither before nor after division. Infinite spirit is neither divided nor divisible.

When the notion of creation 'out of nothing' is examined, it is found to be far less formidable than at first sight it appears. In the world around us at every moment, what did not exist comes to exist. The difference between creation and ordinary efficient causality is that the latter has a subject in which the change takes place while the former has no subject. Until God's existence and causality are accepted, no change whatever begins to be positively intelligible. And even when God's existence and causality are accepted, we have no direct insight into the *how* of any change, any coming to be. We have to accept the fact of change because it is inescapable; but in itself it presents the same problem as does creation.

Creation 'out of nothing' does not mean that 'nothing' is the matter out of which God creates; it means 'not out of something'; that there is in creation no pre-existing matter. When it is said that all the time in the world around us what did not exist comes into existence, the scientific mind might be inclined to question this. From one point of view there is only rearrangement of matter or its components. But to say that such rearrangement involves nothing new is much less than half the story. Corn grows for starving men: nothing new; men of genius and all their works: nothing new; between happiness and misery, true and false, good and bad: no difference, nothing new. Things are specified by their forms, not by their matter, whether matter is understood in the scientific or in the philosophic sense; though it is true that a material *thing* is not matter only, nor form only, but form in matter.

Some scientists formerly objected that coming to be out of nothing is impossible, because science never observes it; now some are saying that science must postulate it. It is also being said that it is scientifically probable that the world had a beginning. But such hypotheses, one way or the other, are of no direct philosophical relevance; even scientifically, they are always open to revision.

The analogy, then, between ordinary efficient causality and creation is striking; and there is the further parallel that the ordinary finite efficient cause is not changed by causing, loses nothing by causing. Nothing passes over or jumps across from cause to effect. The common-sense difficulty suggested by such things as light and heat from the sun is merely apparent; such changes are not true types of efficient causality. In fact, when one reflects how much is new in ordinary causality, it seems to leave very little to distinguish it from creation, and to make it correspondingly easy to allow that creation is possible. The next point to show is that creation is not merely a matter of the remote past, but of the present.

Note on the possibility of an eternal world. Here the word 'eternal' is used in its wider meaning to indicate a world that had no beginning. St Thomas held that it is an article of faith that the world had a beginning; but that philosophically it could not be proved either that the world must have had a beginning or that it need not have had a beginning. One or two modern scholastic philosophers and theologians hold that an eternal world is easier to defend philosophically, and venture to question whether it is really an article of faith that the world had a beginning. For a discussion of these views the reader may be referred to *L'Idée de Création* by A. D. Sertillanges, O.P. (Aubier, Paris, 1945), chapters i and ii. The more common view is that there is no philosophical difficulty about a non-eternal world either from the point of view of the nature of God or from that of the nature of the world. An eternal will to create in no way necessitates an eternal world if the will is that the effect should have a beginning. Even men, in granting jurisdiction for instance, can will an effect to take place from a certain date and not before; though here one has to beware of imagining that God's eternity makes Him exist 'before' time in any temporal sense.

3. *Conservation*

Conservation is not really distinct from creation; the two are distinguished only in the sense that creation looks to the beginning of the world, if it had a beginning, conservation to its continuance; but the same reason is required for the continuance as is required for the beginning. This, however, is not altogether obvious at first sight.

Why does the world go on existing? What is sought is the reason that makes the difference between the world's being something and being nothing. Things in the world depend on finite causes internal and external for beginning to be and continuing to be the *type* of things they are; but if they cease to be one type of thing they forthwith become another type of thing; as things, they do not become absolutely nothing. The reason or cause that makes the difference to the world between being something and being nothing cannot be found in the world as a whole or in any part of it. The whole of creation is necessarily finite and as such dependent for its existence. It is not altogether easy to see at first sight why conservation might not be delegated in some way by God, but St Thomas insists that this is impossible. The ultimate reason he gives is, only God can give existence because only God *is* existence of His very nature; all creatures are not existing of their very nature, but only receive existence. It is true that finite causes also give existence in a way presently to be defined. In doing so they are instruments of God, but in a way that does not exclude God's immediate causality, to which alone is due the fact that all finite agents and their effects are something rather than nothing. It is useless, therefore, to say that all a thing needs in order to exists is existence; for finite existence of its very nature does not explain itself. If one finite thing does not explain itself, the totality of finite things does not explain itself; if the beginning does not explain itself, neither does the continuance; for all the effect is of essentially the same condition, and involves the same dependence.

Conservation is continuous in the sense that the effect is continuous; God's act of conservation is no more continuous than God is. God wills that the world should continue, and so it does continue, and could not continue otherwise. The continuous being which is the world, though it depends on God at every moment, is not thereby essentially new and different at every moment, but is one and the same. The difference induced by persistence in time is accidental only.

It is sometimes said that created things tend by their nature to relapse into nothingness, because all they are is being received from God. St Thomas refuses to talk in this way. It is true that, left to themselves, finite things would be nothing; but their being, as received, is not a tendency into nothing, but on the contrary tends dynamically to its own preservation and, if possible, increase. All being is self-assertive, self-expressive, dynamic, because it is maintained so by God, and because these qualities are inseparable from the very notion of existent being. Even a thing that dies or corrupts, of its nature, and apart from free will, always puts up the best fight it can for as long as it can.

Things depend on causes and conditions internal and external for continuing to be the type of thing they are. This kind of conservation is technically called, not very aptly, indirect conservation. A sheep depends on parent animals for beginning to be, but not, once produced, for continuing to be a sheep. Its sheepness belongs to it and is maintained by various external causes and conditions like heat and nourishment. To provide the sheep with good pasture and keep it away from poisonous pasture is to exercise indirect conservation of it, to help to make the difference between sheep and dead matter. The same is true in its degree of works of art and manufacture. Other effects depend on their causes not only for starting to be but also for continuing to be; for example, the shape of water in a bowl. All this is obvious, but it serves to illustrate how God's causality is exercised in these various cases. God exercises direct conservation of the sheep by making the difference between sheep and nothing. External causes and conditions, themselves directly conserved by God, co-operate with God's direct conservation by helping to make the difference between sheep and dead matter. In the production of new things, whether new substances like a sheep or new accidental differences as in modelling clay, God's causality is called concurrence, and He is called the primary cause; other causes are called secondary or proximate causes, and the relation between the two causes will be discussed in the next section.

St Thomas holds that God could have decreed to create

the world and let it eventually be annihilated; but that there are good reasons for saying that God has decreed never to let the world be annihilated. St Thomas's picture of the 'end of the world' is something of a curiosity. At the 'end of the world', that is, when there are to be no more men, the material world will remain, but will become a sort of museum piece. Plants and animals will become extinct, and matter—apart from human bodies which will remain with or be reunited with human souls—will be resolved into the four elements of earth, air, fire and water. All movement and activity will cease, though the heavenly bodies will remain.[1] Here one has to separate thirteenth-century physics from philosophy; and one may reflect that even twentieth-century physics is not essentially more permanent. It may be mentioned in passing that there is no great difficulty, as St Thomas sees the matter, about human souls getting back human bodies. In the last resort any matter will do; and for a soul to become once more embodied does not necessarily imply the assuming of anything from the graves—or elsewhere—of the world. For St Thomas, as for Aristotle, prime matter has no bulk.

4. *God's concurrence with finite causes*

We now pass to God's co-operation with created causes, and so far as free causes are concerned one might expect in the light of the history of the question to run into difficulties; but I venture to think that the question and its answer can be simplified without distortion.

It might be questioned whether, in finite causality, any co-operation of God is required or possible, because it is difficult to see how two agents, infinite and finite, could

[1] cf. *De Potentia*, 5:7 and 9; *Contra Gentiles*, 4:97.

combine; secondly, because the finite agent, if it has by its very nature the power to produce effects, would seem to be sufficient by itself; and lastly, because it is difficult to see how God could co-operate with free acts without either on the one hand depending on our freedom, or on the other destroying it.

Malebranche held that God alone is the cause of finite effects; that finite causes *seem* to be active, but are in fact only occasions of the production of effects by God. St Thomas insists strongly that finite causes are true causes and not mere occasions. Conservation, as described above, extends to the holding of the agent in existence. If the agent as thus conserved by God were all the cause that is necessary to produce what is new in finite causality, that would be *mediate* concurrence with finite causes on the part of God. If the agent as thus conserved by God is not alone sufficient to produce what is new, so that what is new is the immediate effect of God as well as of the finite cause, this would be called *immediate* concurrence on the part of God. St Thomas holds that the latter is required. All finite existence, as existence, requires the immediate causality of God; for a cause acts according to its nature; and only God is, of His nature, existence.

A finite cause cannot, entirely of itself, give existence; for a finite cause is a nature which is not identical with its existence but only receives existence. The office of the finite cause is therefore to co-operate in producing natures which receive existence from God. I paraphrase St Thomas:[1] 'Existence is the effect proper to the first cause, God; and all other agents produce existence in so far as the power of God acts through them as instruments. Finite agents particularize and specify the action of God, and produce as their

[1] *Contra Gentiles*, 3:66.

own proper effects those perfections which delimit existence
to such and such a nature.'

This unique co-operation of finite and infinite causes
needs further description. God gives existence, that which
makes the difference between something and nothing. The
finite cause co-operates by specifying the nature which
receives the existence: a round nail makes a round hole; a
rose produces a rose. This, however, does not mean that God
gives the existence only, the finite agent the essence only,
still less that God gives the substance, the finite agents the
accidents. Both agents produce the *thing*, essence and existence, but in different ways. God produces existence by His
own power; the finite cause produces existence in virtue of
being God's instrument for its production. A rose produces
a rose rather than a dandelion in virtue of being a rose. But
even here the finite cause is instrumental to some extent, in
so far as it could not have its own nature, nor use it, except
in subordination to God. An analogy would be a painter
who makes his own brush. That there is any painting at all
is due to the painter; that the strokes are of such a thickness
is due to the brush; yet the whole effect is due immediately
to both painter and brush. A mere brush does not of its
nature paint a picture; but we say a rose does of its nature
produce a rose. This is because the nature of a rose is the
permanent instrument of God for producing existence, and
rose-existence.

From different points of view God may be conceived as
an agent external to the creature, and as internal to it. He is
external in so far as He is adequately distinct from the
creature; He is internal in so far as by His immensity the
whole creature and every part of it is equally and immediately the effect of God.

This concurrence of God is immediate and simultaneous

with the agent in producing the effect. The concurrence falls on what is new in finite causality; that is, on the effect. Sometimes the effect arises within the person or thing acting, as in an act of intellect or will, or a tree growing. Sometimes the effect arises in a separate thing, as in painting, or cutting down a tree. I paraphrase St Thomas's summary of the matter:

> Thus God is a cause of every kind of action; because He gives the power to act, conserves it, and applies it to action; and because every other active power acts in virtue of His active power. And if we add further that God and His active power are identical, and that He is within everything, not as part of its essence but as holding it in existence, it will be seen that God is immediately operative in every agent, including the agency of will and of nature.[1]

The above theory may be applied to God's concurrence with acts of free will as follows: (i) Every human action is a moral action. This is a well-established principle of moral philosophy, and amounts to no more than saying that if a human action is not morally bad, it is morally good. Of course, a good human action can fall short of perfection in a number of ways. A human action as a moral action is subject to the general principle of goodness and badness, that goodness is completeness, fullness of being, badness as such is always defect, falling away, failing to fulfil an idea or ideal. This too is a well-established and completely satisfactory principle. More will be said about it in dealing with the problem of evil. (ii) Before acting, a man has the power to produce a morally good action. This must be so, otherwise if he produced a morally bad action it would not be imputable to him. (iii) If he chooses and does a good action, the

[1] *De Potentia*, 3:7; cf. *Contra Gentiles*, 3:67.

causes are God and the free human will; if he chooses and does a bad action, the cause of the badness as such is the deficient human will alone. The same applies to good actions so far as they are morally imperfect. Thus, whether the action is good or bad, choice and performance are in the power of the free man.

Already St Augustine was quite clear about the privative, defective character of badness as such. I paraphrase *De Civitate Dei*, 12:7:

> Let no one seek an efficient productive cause of a bad will; the cause is not efficient but deficient; it does not produce something, but fails to produce something. To begin to have a bad will is to decline from what is full and complete to what is incomplete. To look for the causes of such defects, when the causes are, as I have said, not efficient but deficient, is like trying to see darkness or hear silence; and yet both darkness and silence are known to us, the one through the eyes, the other through the ears; not indeed through their own natures, but through their want of natures.

In this analysis, the human action is taken not materially but 'formally', that is, considering its intelligibility; and that is the right way to take it because it is the way everything has to be considered when we want to know what it is. A bad action may cause a great deal of fuss and upheaval; materially it may bring all sorts of things into existence; it may have immediately the same external effects as a good action; but nevertheless, considered in its degree of intelligibility, which is the same as its degree of goodness and of being, it is a privation and not something positive.

Thus a free action is considered as a human action, its agent a man. If one wished to analyse it further, considering how the object first presents itself to the intellect, how the intellect apprehends it, how the will goes out to it, at first indeliberately and then deliberately and finally with full acceptance—all this would be interesting as a piece of psychology, but for the immediate purpose not directly necessary. It is easy to forget that a human action is not an act of intellect nor of will but of a man. This much, however, is relevant, that if it be asked whether the will, in going out to a specified object and identifying itself with it, thereby changes, I should reply that it does; not as agent but as patient, as receiving a new actuation. It has been maintained in various ways by various authors that the consent of the will adds nothing to the will. I do not agree with this conclusion. The grain of truth it contains is that the will *as agent* does not change. One thing is certain, an act of will changes a man. By it he makes his own, identifies himself with, an object good or bad. If the badness is such as to turn him away from his last end, this deprives him—to confine ourselves to the natural order—of his free relation to God and induces a new relation away from God. Relations are sometimes thought of as the slenderest of entities. This is strange. They have a remarkable toughness and universality. In God they are strong enough to constitute divine persons; in this world they are strong enough to bind men to God.

5. *Why God created the world*

Why does God create the world? The answer, when properly grasped, can throw a flood of light on all that can be known about God and the world by reason, unifying all in a sweep of thought only a Dante could express worthily. The final reason why God creates the world is His own goodness. That is the thread that runs through creation from

first to last, from its first going out from God to its last return to Him in the perfect fulfilment of His plan.

To say that God's goodness is the reason for creation
might seem at first to mean that God creates simply in
order to give men the chance of sharing His happiness. That
reason is true as far as it goes, but it is not the whole truth
nor the deepest aspect of the matter. Consider again the
comparison already mentioned of a photograph. A father
has a small son he loves; he has his son photographed and
distributes copies to his friends and relations. He values the
photographs and expects others to value them because they
are likenesses of someone he loves. This comparison may
provide the first and basic reason why God creates the
world. Knowing His own infinite perfection, He loves it
with infinite love; and because He loves it, and because
creation is possible, He wants His perfection to be diffused
and manifested. God loves His creatures because they are
images of Himself.

This conclusion sounds simple enough, but there have
been philosophers who did not see it clearly. In the seven-
teenth century the eminent theologian Leonard Lessius put
the matter somewhat out of focus by stressing the reason of
God's desiring the external glory due to Him, as though
that could be for God an end in itself. This wrong emphasis
led astray not a few philosophers and theologians, even after
the Vatican Council, following St Thomas, had reaffirmed
the right perspective. In the middle of the last century one
or two German theologians fell into error by maintaining
that God's reason for creating is simply and solely the good
of creatures; otherwise, so it was imagined, God's purpose
in creating would be self-centred in a way it cannot be. The
difficulty is groundless, as has been explained. God in
creating looks to no gain for Himself; His happiness is infinite

and can know no increase. Secondly, it is impossible to say that any reason apart from God Himself is the reason for creation; for if it were so, God would be dependent on something other than Himself, whereas He cannot be dependent in any way. Finally, God is and must be the centre to which all else is referred; creatures are not the centre; their centre is God.

The difficulty that is at first felt that if God's infinite goodness is the object of His will as *not* creating, something else must be the object of His will as creating, is one more consequence of our finite-mindedness. Creation adds no further perfection to infinite perfection, does not increase the object of an infinite will.

St Thomas says that things come out from God and return to God *circulatione quadam*, by a sort of circular movement. On the way out, the matter is seen from the point of view of God's intention, His reason for the making of the world. It is God's goodness, that is, not mere benevolence, but His infinite perfection in all its aspects—love, wisdom, justice, mercy. This infinite perfection must be the primary object of God's will in creating. It cannot be so under the aspect of infinite good to be obtained or produced; it can only be under the aspect of infinite good to be diffused and manifested by finite participations.

Now consider the way back, the function of creatures. This must correspond to the reason why God made them. The primary end of creatures is not their own well-being for its own sake, but their goodness as embodying and manifesting the goodness of God. That is what creatures are for, man included. 'It is not the virtue of thy soul that makes thee happy,' says St Augustine, 'but He who has given thee the virtue, who has inspired thee to will, and has given thee the power to do so.'

God draws all things to Himself like a magnet. When we say it is the highest kind of love to love other people for their own sakes, what we really mean is that we ought to love other people for God's sake. This idea is neither vague nor very difficult. To love another person for his own sake means to wish him well; to wish that he may find his fulfilment and happiness. This people do by loving God and tending towards Him, becoming more united to Him, more like Him. If I love another person with the highest kind of love, I treat him in such a way as to make it easy for him to serve God and reach his final end. Thus from another angle may be seen what conclusions follow from the truth that God is the centre of all things.

To return to the comparison of a photograph. Between God and man there is a greater difference than between a man and a piece of paper that bears his image. From revelation we learn that God has been pleased to make men not mere remote images of Himself, but His sons. By supernatural grace we share God's divine life; a pure gift that overtops mere human nature immeasurably. Now suppose that the photograph has the power, as we have, to change the image of the person it represents. Suppose the living photograph freely and knowingly distorts the image, turning it into a hideous caricature and refusing to be mended. There is nothing the father can do about it except regretfully throw it away. It makes a mockery of the purpose for which it was made. Suppose again that another person takes the photograph of the father's son and makes it hideous. What will the father think of such a person? There is the obligation of love of one's neighbour in a nutshell.

The happiness of rational creatures, though it is God's will for them, is not the absolutely ultimate end and test of the success of God's plan in creation, for it is willed and desired conditionally, the condition being that men do not freely and obstinately spoil the image of God in themselves. Even if they do, in the words of G. M. Hopkins, 'God gets His glory'; for His justice is manifested in the unrepentant. The final end of creation can never be frustrated, for it is God Himself: and everything in creation shows forth God in one way or another. Nothing in creation can be sheer loss except to the creature who will not have God and stays so through death into eternity. Finally, the purpose of lower creatures is easily seen to fit into the same scheme. They, too, by their natures reflect God, look to God, tend to God by being what they are meant to be. They are made for men's needs of soul and body, to go along with him by enriching him and helping him to know and serve God.

6. *Providence*

By divine providence is understood God's eternal plan for the world, directing it to its end. That God has such a plan, known in complete detail and executed infallibly, is evident from His attributes of wisdom and power. All that happens does so exactly as He wills to effect or wills to allow, and not otherwise. God's knowledge of creation as directing it to its end is the highest aspect of His knowledge of creation. As St Thomas often points out, 'the final perfection of everything consists in its attainment of its end'; and what is true of each part is eminently true of the whole plan. The whole plan is ruled by its unity; its details cannot be appreciated in their relation to the whole until the whole is seen complete. All the details of creation are, in their different ways, means to the end, but the differences are important; God does not treat persons as mere means. He gives them the dignity of directing themselves freely to their end, with all the help necessary to do this. Their end then becomes God's means; and its dignity is thereby enhanced and given the final and inseparable perfection of all finite good, that of being subordinate to God. To say, 'Will you help me with my plan?' is not to treat persons merely as means. It must never be lost sight of that God's will, whether effective of good or permissive of evil, leaves human freedom absolutely intact. What is true of creation as a whole is true in its measure of each human life. The whole of creation looks forward for its explanation, as the finished portrait rules the artist's brush-strokes; and while we can speculate about the direction and meaning of history only with great reserve, we can more confidently read individual lives, especially our own, when we look back. Whatever our lives amount to, whatever we may come to be, we can always stop and say that all that has happened up to this moment has been willed and allowed by God for the manifestation of His goodness; all that has happened up to this moment is now part of the means for me to give God the glory He now wants me to give Him. From the point of view of God's will for the world, there is no such thing as chance.

7. *Miracles*

A miracle is an effect of God outside the range of natural causes. Usually, but not universally, it would be sufficient to say, 'outside the range of existing natural causes'. St Thomas does not restrict miracles to observable effects, but includes, e.g., Transubstantiation; but it will be convenient here to consider only observable miracles. If God exists and His causality is universal and immediate and, though working normally through existing natural causes, is, absolutely speaking, entirely independent of them, it is immediately evident that God can work miracles if He can have a sufficient reason for doing so. That He can have such a reason may be known from the actual occurrence of miracles; and so observable miracles may be defined by reference to actual ones, as effects of God outside the range of natural causes, their purpose being usually to guarantee some truth or commend some person.

This description is gathered, as I said, from actual miracles; but actual miracles are here used only to provide a working definition; I am not here concerned to show that miracles do take place. It needs to be shown that miracles as thus defined can take place, and also that they can be recognizable. The first point can be shown briefly by saying that God can produce any effect that is not impossible to Him, not self-contradictory, not out of keeping with any of His attributes; and that such are observable miracles as we have defined them. Difficulties of detail will be considered presently.

Secondly, an observable miracle could be recognizable as such; it could be possible to exclude every alternative explanation. For this to happen, the following combination of circumstances would be needed:

(i) an observer who holds that God exists and that His nature and causality are as they have been described above. If a person rejects this position, he will exclude the possibility of miracle *a priori*, and will in the last resort accept any explanation, however unspecified or difficult, rather than admit that an event is miraculous; (ii) an effect known to be outside the range of (at least available) natural causes; (iii) a religious context in which some doctrine or person claiming to represent God is associated with the event; (iv) the exclusion of the hypothesis that God has permitted some evil spirit—supposing such to exist—to produce a preternatural effect.

These would seem to be the essentials and sufficient for the recognition of a miracle. In the concrete the circumstances would be greatly strengthened as evidence if alleged miracles were multiplied in the context of the same doctrine or body of doctrine and the same type of person associated with it. It is claimed, then, that these circumstances can combine to produce ample certainty in the recognition of a miracle. It needs to be stressed that the matter is always a concrete one, and depends on the convergence of evidence, like any other concrete event. Miracles are addressed to men, and men can be shrewd enough to know when the evidence is sufficient to produce certainty.

It remains to consider some of the difficulties which may be felt on the subject, even by those who do not rule out the possibility of miracle *a priori*.

(i) *If miracles happen, it is all up with science and the laws of nature. Unaccountable exceptions may occur at any time to confuse the observer.*—On the contrary, unless we can be certain of the relevant laws of nature, we can never be certain of a miracle's being outside their range. Further, miracles, from the nature of the case, do not occur haphazard, but arise only in recognizable religious contexts; otherwise there would be no good reason for beginning to suspect that they were miracles.

(ii) *The 'laws of nature' are only hypotheses, liable to revision; therefore we can never be sure that an exception to them is miraculous.*—This is true of some laws of nature, but most people would allow exceptions. Further, most laws of nature are not completely superseded by the progress of science, but only explained more clearly and in a wider context. For a man four days dead and corrupting to be raised to life would be allowed by most people to be outside the range of nature. Similarly in such a case as that attributed to St John

Vianney a little over a hundred years ago, for a granary containing a few handfuls of corn to be suddenly filled half full without human agency.

(iii) *If it is true that God manifests Himself in the world by creation, what need is there for Him to do it by means of miracles as well?*—God manifests His existence and much about His attributes by creation. But He can, if He sees fit, manifest this anew and in more striking ways for the benefit of particular people. But, much more fundamentally, if there are truths about God which are not available to natural reason through the contemplation of nature, and if God wills to reveal them, then the only possible way of doing so is by preternatural means, that is by miracle. At the very least there would need to be preternaturally infused knowledge given to men. This God gave to the Prophets in the Old Testament, guaranteeing their message by prophecy and other miracles. Christ as God-man is a living miracle, and His supernatural message was guaranteed by further miracles observable by others. And the same type of guarantee of the same message is, the Catholic holds, not infrequent in the world today.

(iv) *A miracle implies that God is putting to rights a world He has left imperfect: surely this is not worthy of Him.*—The basic purpose of miracles is not to perfect a world imperfect in the natural order. This was not the purpose of Christ's miracles of healing. The good they did to people was not just for its own sake, but to reveal anew and in a special way the goodness of God, and much more, to guarantee Christ's doctrine and person.

(v) *God could provide special revelation simply by the acknowledged goodness and holiness of His saints and prophets.*—If the revelation is supernatural, it could not be conveyed to the saints and prophets except by miracle. For the rest, it is not easy to tell the true prophet from the false, the true saints from the pseudo-saints and from men good according to their lights who are not God's accredited messengers. So-called prophets speak with contradictory voices, and the ordinary man is at a loss which to believe. He knows they cannot all be right, and He thinks that God is interested in men knowing the truth. Miracles would be one means of meeting this difficulty.

(vi) *Unknown forces could explain all alleged miracles.*—This objection is best considered as a comment on the miracles *de facto* accepted by Christians, those of Christ, those of Lourdes and many more. Perhaps in isolation the 'unknown forces' argument could be sustained without absurdity, no matter what the facts in a particular case; some would be willing to accept it even in the case of a man four days dead and corrupting. But the physical fact is only part of the evidence which depends, as has been said, on a convergence of circumstances which can be amply sufficient to warrant a wholly reasonable assent.

The question of miracles as historical facts is outside the scope of this essay.

8. *The problem of evil*

The object of God's will can be nothing but good, namely, His own infinite goodness; and that, too, is the object of His will as creator. The will to create the world includes the will-to-produce good and the will-to-allow evil. Both these are included in the act by which God wills infinite good. The effects of this will in the world are, of course, finite.

It is generally thought that the goodness of God's will-to-permit evil is, in the natural order, the truth about God that is furthest removed from our insight, and this is probably true. But, to repeat what can scarcely be said too often, to suppose that in principle we ought to have insight into this truth, and that in the order of natural reason it cannot be known for certain until we do have insight, would be to have gone badly astray on the fundamentals of method of a sound natural theology.

The next observation is that if God's allowing of evil to take its course is the deepest of natural mysteries, one might expect that this would be a point where natural mystery would be joined by supernatural revelation, and so it is. The crucifixion of Christ is an affirmation before the eyes of the world of God's will to permit evil: not an answer to the question 'Why?' but an acceptance of the fact by God made man, and an invitation to us to join Him in acceptance. Does revelation make the problem harder or easier? It is not very evident what the answer should be. Those who accept revelation by divine faith have no hesitation in accepting this part of it. They accept it with heart and head; they see the reasonableness of accepting it; they love God for revealing it and for not revealing any more. But revelation presents a fact that would not otherwise be a necessary hypothesis; I mean the eternal ruin of Satan and his associates who said, 'We will not serve.' This can be taken into account even when thinking the matter out at the natural level. Every fact can be a help to right thinking. But it is only fair to point out that those who do not accept the whole of revelation are not in a very strong position for appreciating what can be said about this part of revelation. For those to whom the crucifixion of Christ means little or nothing, hell cannot be seen in its right perspective.

As with every other mystery, natural and supernatural, it can be claimed that there is no evident contradiction. It cannot be shown that God cannot will to allow evil to take

its course. Difficulties and misunderstandings should be
removed as far as possible; and this is best done by putting
the facts objectively and in the right perspective so far as
human thought and language will allow. The problem of
evil sometimes suffers badly in this respect. What is required
is to see the matter, as far as we can, from God's point of
view.

First a glance at the history of the problem. It is not easy
to sum up the Greeks on this question. But if to hold the
ultimate intelligibility of the universe is to hold its ultimate
goodness, most of the great Greek philosophers would
qualify for the name of tempered optimists; and it is a fact
that most if not all the reasons—save those drawn from
revelation—offered by Christian philosophers for the understanding of evil, may be found first in the Greeks. No doubt
this optimism is due in part to a sort of intellectual first
fervour which tended in time to issue in diverging views,
disillusionment in some, stronger conviction in others,
sometimes even at the same period in the same school:
contrast, for instance, the two late Stoics, Marcus Aurelius
and Epictetus. But no philosophic optimist need be ashamed
of the names of—to look no further—Plato, Aristotle and
Plotinus.

The chief opinions of later Western philosophers on the
problem of evil may be divided thus:

(i) *Pessimism:* the opinion that in the world evil so far
exceeds good that it would be better for the world not to
exist; that the world cannot have been created by a good
God, but arises from the blind impulse of an irrational force
immanent in the world. Thus, for example, Schopenhauer.

(ii) *Dualism:* the opinion that there are two ultimate and
irreducible principles, one good, one bad. Thus the Manichaeans and the Gnostics, for both of which sects matter was

the principle of evil. Schelling postulates two such opposite principles, one of which he calls the principle of light, the other the principle of darkness.

(iii) *Optimism* is chiefly associated with the name of Leibniz. God by a moral necessity creates the best of all possible worlds. It is impossible for God to remove any evil from this world without thereby producing a worse evil. To this opinion a number of other philosophers and theologians have at various times inclined to some degree: Abelard, Wiclif, Malebranche, Rosmini.

The analysis of the situation traditional in Christian philosophy is that of which all the main lines were laid down by St Augustine in his controversy with the Manichaeans. Briefly it is as follows:

1. God wills to use what is called physical evil not as an end in itself, but as a means to good.
2. God wills moral evil neither as an end in itself nor as a means to good, but wills to allow it to take its course.
3. The ultimate object of God's will as thus directed to the world is in both cases entirely good, namely, the diffusion and manifestation in finite things of His infinite perfections.
4. The effect of His will for the world, its course and its final outcome, He knows with certainty and brings to pass infallibly.
5. It cannot be shown that God's will as thus directed to the world is out of keeping with any of His attributes, goodness, holiness or any other.

Many clues can be given to recommend this conclusion, but they do not give direct insight, and in that sense do not claim to solve the problem.

These five statements may now be examined more closely.

1. By physical evil is meant every kind of evil except sin.

Physical evil therefore includes physical and mental suffering in this life; also death; and the punishment of evildoers after death. The theory is, then, that in so far as these things are bad, God's will is not directed to them for their own sakes, but only as means to produce some good. This good is always ultimately the manifestation of His perfections and, with one exception—the final reprobation of the unrepentant—it contains the means or at least the opportunity of good for those who suffer.[1]

The term physical *evil* is a weighted one; it contains the suggestion that physical evil and moral evil are somehow on a level. But it is convenient to retain the term, with the caution that, as will be presently shown, physical evil when compared with moral evil is evil only by remote analogy.

The question may be asked, why are physical and mental pain and death called evils? In general it is taken for granted that they are so, but it is worth while to ask why; whether it is right to think of all defect and suffering as bad; in what sense any defect and suffering is bad. The question is, what is our standard? Evil is rightly defined as a priva-

---

[1] Evil, as has been said before, is a defect in a good nature or in a complex of natures, inducing, from the formal point of view, a defective situation. A worm-eaten apple is to that extent a bad apple; a body with a cancer is to that extent a bad body. One can easily be misled into thinking that more matter means more being, more goodness, more intelligibility; this is often not so. If a hand is too big or too little, it is the same from the point of view of the goodness of a human hand. It induces less goodness, less intelligibility, less being. A hundred tons of rubble dumped in Westminster Abbey makes, in the situation, less goodness, less intelligibility, less being; the same hundred tons dumped elsewhere could help to level a field. Goodness, being, intelligibility, are measured by the mind, not by the amount of matter. This theory, a direct consequence of the existence of God, has nothing whatever to do with the false theory that pain is non-real or imaginary. Pain is perfectly real and positive as a sensation—in the suffering body too much so. A bad thing is a thing with a defect in it; but the defect may be induced by something positive like the excess of feeling called pain, or by the lack of feeling called insensibility.

tion in a nature; that is, the absence of some good which a nature ought to have. But what *ought* a nature to have? How do we know what it ought to have? We imagine the perfect type of the individual rose, rabbit, human body, and think that when it falls notably below the ideal standard it is to that extent bad. If a human body has pain we say it is a bad thing, something wrong, physical evil. But the question needs to be asked, what right we have to judge these things simply and solely in terms of our ideal standard for the individual specimen. We have an initial right, and a good reason, namely, that each individual nature tends to its own good; it has a natural appetite to it, and of necessity; the frustration of this natural urge is reasonably said to be a bad thing for the individual specimen. But this natural tendency in the individual specimen is an extremely limited aspect of the thing; and if the thing is limited to its individual aspect, this distorts the picture even of the thing's nature. I believe that the inclination to see individual specimens of physical things, including the human body, as things in their own right, is largely an anthropomorphism in the sense that we reflect on to material things what is comparatively true in ourselves, namely, that men are persons, things in their own right, and, under God, ends in themselves. All material creation, including human bodies, is not an end in itself; how much truer that any individual material thing, even a human body, is not an end in itself. People speak of the perfect rose or rabbit or human body; but the individual cannot be understood completely except in relation to the species; nor the species except in relation to the whole of nature; nor the whole of nature except in relation to man; nor man except in relation to God. The whole of material nature is constituted by a hierarchy of tensions between the claims of lower and higher elements, individual and species, species and the rest of nature, nature and man; and finally man is constituted, his very creature-hood is defined by, the tension between finite and infinite. These tensions combine to produce the good thing called creation. Without the tension between rational creatures and God, no intelligible creation of rational beings would be possible. Without the tensions within material creation, and between material creation and spirit, it is very hard to see how any material creation would be possible.

These are reflections which suggest themselves at this point when we are declaring and analysing what is meant by saying that God, in producing the good He intends to produce, can and does use what is called physical evil, as a means to good. They suggest that even what seems to be the simplest item in the situation, that physical evil is rightly so called, is not so evident as at first sight it seemed. I should prefer to call it simply tension or stress, the underlying principle, as Heraclitus saw it, of all reality and all good in the universe. The purpose of physical evil is one only, to give man the opportunity of full creaturehood, of recogniz-ing in the world and manifesting in himself the perfection of God. It is good if it does this, bad if it does not; and we are not in a position to say that it does not, nor that there is any suffering that is not ultimately productive of good even for the sufferer, with the exception of the eternal loss of God. If anyone imagines he could propose a better scheme of things, that could only mean a scheme of things that would better help men to God in the way He wants men to be helped. But we cannot do more than surmise about the details of the way God wants men to be helped to Him, though we can apply general principles with fair confidence.

From revelation we learn that man was at first free from pain and death, and that these came into the world as the result of sin. This can hardly mean that man was entirely free from all pain before the Fall, because his trial was a stress laid upon him. He became aware of the tension of his creaturehood, and of the obligation he was under of choosing in the face of every alternative the God he knew only indirectly. Apart from this, his body was by a special gift of God exempt from the stress of being simply part of the material world and meeting its hazards; exempt, too, from the irrational bias towards the material called concupiscence; and exempt from the darkening of mind and weakening of will caused by sin. His natural intellect was enlightened and his will strengthened by grace which made him a sharer in God's life yet able to lose it. With all these advantages the first man was tested and failed. This suggests strongly that his testing was objectively very severe. It seems to me very probable that the testing of the first man involved a stress of soul more severe than anything we can now experience. In any case, some stress there must have been, and it may be seen as an example of what, in fact, is found in creation from first to last, in things great and small, that God has willed that in this world all good should be produced through conflict; the greater the conflict the greater the opportunity of good; but also the greater the likelihood of failure where free wills are concerned. As a result of the Fall of man, his body reverted to its purely natural condition of sharing the hazards of the rest of material nature. He lost his exemption from concupiscence; his mind became less clear and his will weaker; and he lost the supernatural life of grace, but, by a further act of grace, God was pleased to give him the means of recovering it.

Thus man now entered a different sphere of tensions, the one in which we now live; in which there is more chance of failure in soul and mind and body, but also full opportunities of repair—redemption for his soul, revelation for his mind, and doctors for his body. And lest he should still be dejected, God did all this for him bountifully, and Himself plunged into this world and without need, out of love, shared it with him at what seems its worst, and perhaps is its best, to the utmost pitch possible for God made man, to death, even the death of the cross.

Why do the innocent suffer? Any answer to this question must take account of two transcendences: the first that, as is explained in the next section, physical suffering and moral evil are not commensurable: physical suffering is not the evil of the human person as such. Secondly, eternal life in the possession of God is not commensurable with this life. This reduces physical suffering to its proper proportions. What can be said about it for certain is that in all cases God produces through suffering a greater good than suffering is an evil. It would be absurd to expect to be able to trace out in detail and to the end how this is so in any particular case. As St Thomas reminds us, 'the order of things, their place in the scheme of divine providence, their relations to one another and the way they are directed to their end, can be known to us only in a slight degree; because the plan of divine providence is beyond the range of our knowledge'.[1] But the best answer to the question would seem to be: let the innocent speak for themselves. Human nature has been wholly innocent in only two people of adult age, Christ and His Mother. Christ gives His answer from the cross, His Mother from the foot of the cross. Next to them, the saints are those who have given their lives to striving for innocence, and for them that meant striving for union through love with the redemptive love of Christ crucified. Other men and women are innocent in so far as they have

[1] *Contra Gentiles*, 4:1.

the mind of Christ. With these for witness, one does not turn for a better answer to the sinner and the whiner. The saints have no respect for the wisdom of those who want to do their grumbling for them.

There remains the suffering of children too young to sin, and this would seem to be one of the hardest cases, even for those who see the mistake of making any man, woman or child the centre of the universe, and who accept entirely, with heart and head, the two transcendences I have mentioned above. Suffering cannot harm innocent children as persons, that is, in their moral natures, at the time; and later the memory or effects of their suffering cannot harm them except in so far as they freely and culpably allow it to do so. There is also the consideration, not a negligible one, that the capacity to suffer in the full sense comes only with the full use of reason. The Catholic is able to add from revelation the solidarity of the human race which forfeited, as a race, the privileges possessed before the Fall, one of which was immunity from the physical hazards of life. On the final assessment the answer will be, in philosophy, that the suffering of innocent children ultimately produces in the universe a compensating good the nature of which we can only conjecture; and in ordinary life the Christian mother of suffering children, for all her grief, is still happy to profess her unshaken faith in a God of infinite love, and to find comfort in union with the Mother of Christ, the Mother of Sorrows.

On the question of the suffering of animals the best reply would seem to be that we do not know what they feel, and have therefore no right to draw conclusions from it. Newman suggested that the consciousness of animals is like a dream-world, and this is very likely, since their consciousness is not reflexive. Their reactions and cries are no safe index of feeling as we understand it. A baby that is slightly hungry or slightly uncomfortable will scream as though it were being murdered.

I do not think it would be very profitable to speculate here on what, if any, was the effect of the Fall on the animal world and the rest of creation apart from man.

2. *God wills moral evil neither as an end in itself nor as a means to good, but wills to allow it to take its course.* God does not and cannot will the sinful actions of creatures even as means to the production of good. The reason is that whereas physical evil does not involve aversion from God, moral evil does. God cannot therefore create a world in which there is sin, *in order that* thereby His justice and mercy may be manifested; but a world in which, in fact, there is sin is a world in which, in fact, His justice and mercy can be manifested; and, sin being supposed, such manifestation is good, and can be the object of God's will. It cannot be too much stressed that God's will to allow sin to take its course is not merely not the willing of sin; much more, sin, as aversion from God, is the object of God's aversion; and if the sin becomes absolute, of His absolute aversion. In this life sin can be repaired by mercy leading to repentance; but if there is no repentance, then sin in the full sense, mortal sin as it is called, cannot have any other issue than total banishment from God and from all enjoyment of the order of good.

Here it is in place to state the relation between physical evil and moral evil. The difference is so fundamental that, by comparison with moral evil, physical evil is evil only by remote analogy. Moral evil totally transcends physical evil. Physical evil, no matter how multiplied, can never equal in badness the smallest moral evil. The reason is, once more, that moral evil is by its very nature a lie against God, a denial of Him or of His nature. Even if it does not amount to aversion from God, rejection of Him as our last end, it still involves a withholding from God of some part of the total acknowledgment due, that He is the supreme good, and our supreme good.

The words of Newman are well known, that it would be better for the whole human race to perish in extreme agony than for a person to tell one small lie or steal one farthing. I do not think we are justified in illustrating principles by means of suppositions of this kind. It is not for us to make such suppositions and assume that they are valid; we do not know that they necessarily follow from the principle. Nevertheless, apart from the illustration, the principle itself is entirely true, namely, that moral evil totally transcends physical evil. More real illustrations would be the actual example of saints and martyrs, whose numbers never fail. Their lives are a living acceptance of the truth that sin and suffering are not commensurable; a truth their nearness to God enables them to see with ever-increasing clearness. Without this truth, human life does not make sense; to reject it is to live irrationally, to attempt to untwine one's creaturehood. Or again, one may imagine those who have reached their last end in God, looking back and seeing their lives by comparison with eternity, their sufferings by comparison with their possession of God. They can only smile to think that their sufferings, whatever they were, ever seemed important.

The best of mankind have always accepted the transcendence of moral values. It was the proud banner of Socrates and of Plato, and was accepted by Aristotle as an acknowledged essential of human life, in spite of the privileged position he assigned to the life of contemplation, and in spite of his obscurity about the immortality of the soul. It is accepted today, but the question, 'What is bodily and mental

well-being as a function of human goodness?' would pro-
voke a good deal of puzzlement and diverging replies, and
the Christian may fairly be challenged with the question,
'What, then, is the metaphysical status of doctors?' If a
great mystic like St Teresa of Avila could take as her motto
aut pati aut mori—either let me suffer or let me die—and yet
thought it allowable and even a duty to seek remedies in
sickness, what conclusions does this require concerning the
relations of soul and body, God and man? This question
deserves a longer answer than can be given here, but briefly,
if God's action in the world is such as has been described
above, then evidently if there are lawful remedies and
medical skills, God is at work in these just as much as in the
sicknesses they attempt to cure; and this is taken for granted
and seems good enough to ordinary Christians. Creaturehood in this world is loving God and recognizing and doing
His will; and the care of health of mind and body would
seem to be part of the process of the repair of the Fall of man
willed by God through Christ. To work this field of speculation further would be out of proportion here.

3. *The ultimate object of God's will as thus directed to the
world is good, namely, the diffusion and manifestation in finite
things of His infinite perfection.* This by itself would not be very
difficult for human reason to accept. But in addition we
learn from revelation that the merits of Christ, the honour
given by Him to God, is beyond comparison greater than
the honour withheld from God by sin; further, that those
who live the life of supernatural grace are incorporated in
this life of Christ; and even in the purely natural order,
good, in spite of appearances, is far more productive of
further good than evil is of evil. All good, like the human
body, tends to repair its own defects.

What evil is left in the universe on the final count? Only

the bad will of those who have chosen to cut themselves off from God, and the plight in which they inevitably place themselves. Basically, hell is simply a part of nature. Souls are naturally immortal, and any that choose exclusion from God introduce into themselves an internal conflict between their nature and their free will. They have denied that God is their good, denied their creaturehood, so that their selves and all that surrounds them are no longer able to do them good, but only to make them suffer.

To sum up: in this world the so-called evil in nature helps to produce the total good which is the order of nature. Pain in man is a natural consequence of his inclusion in the order of nature. It serves to repair the order of justice for his own sins and those of others; it can be a means of self-training and increased union with God; it is at once an instrument of divine justice and divine mercy, enabling men to expiate their sins in ways far less rigorous than justice could demand. If there had been no sin there would have been no bodily suffering; but it does not follow that there would have been no suffering at all, for the essential stress of creaturehood would have been ever-present. Moral evil itself can be the occasion of great good to men. Apart from its being the occasion of manifesting the justice of God, it can manifest also His mercy which is offered to all no matter what their offences. The repentant, as St Thomas beautifully says, generally rise up from their sins more fervent, more humble and more careful than before they sinned.

Furthermore, the sins of others are the opportunity of many virtues and especially of heroic virtues; of values which could not otherwise be obtained. Tyranny and persecution are opposition from one's own species, and this is specially hard; persecution that would do violence to the victim's conscience is opposition from one's own species to

one's own last end, the hardest of all to bear. To bear it for
the love of God and not deny Him is heroic sanctity. To list
the good that would be lost if there were no physical and
mental stress and no sin, would be an endless task.

Experience and the world's literature bear constant
witness to the fact that the highest values are occasioned by
suffering and not otherwise; that suffering is the spur of love
and its only test. An anthology could easily be made of the
unconscious witness borne by non-religious, non-Christian
writers to the Christian view of suffering. Let one small
example suffice. Thomas Hardy described Egdon Heath as
'A place perfectly accordant with man's nature—neither
ghastly, hateful, nor ugly; neither commonplace, unmean-
ing nor tame; but, like man, slighted and enduring'. This,
I have read, was Gustav Holst's ideal of beauty, which he
sought to embody in his tone-poem, *Egdon Heath*. If beauty
attaches to what is slighted and enduring, and if such is
man's condition, then there is no greater beauty in human
things than Christ crucified, the revelation of God to man,
God and man in one. Seldom if ever have art, poetry and
music risen to greater heights than in celebrating the Cross
of Christ, *arbor decora et fulgida*, that fair and shining tree.
Suffering, rightly understood, is simply an aspect of
creaturehood in its endless range and beauty; and those who
will be creatures will find God.

The above account of the problem of evil is based on the
principles handed down from St Augustine. But the reader
may have noticed more than traces of another principle,
which has been proposed in recent times, and used at least
implicitly by a number of recent writers: the theory, namely,
that it may well be metaphysically, that is, absolutely,
impossible for God to create a world of free creatures not

merely without the possibility of physical and moral evil, but without their actual occurrence. I refer to the suggestions put forward by Fr Joseph Rickaby, S.J., in a short article in *The Month* for November 1898, entitled *The Greek Theory of Necessity: a speculation on the origin of evil*, and reprinted as an appendix in the same author's *In An Indian Abbey* (1919). In Fr Rickaby's words:

> The hypothesis is briefly this, that creation without evil is a contradiction in terms: that evil is a natural and necessary incident of all created good: that if God chooses to create at all, He must permit evil to be in creation, and that this . . . is no more an infringement of divine omnipotence than is the impossibility of God's creating a triangle, the angles of which, taken together, should be equal to anything else than two right angles.

This theory seems to me to have received less philosophical and theological attention than it deserves. There have been one or two criticisms, none conclusive that I have seen. I wish to say that I accept the theory as a probable hypothesis in the following terms: either that it is metaphysically, i.e. absolutely, impossible for God to create a world of free creatures without physical and moral evil; or at least that certain uniquely excellent and irreplaceable values cannot be obtained without physical and moral evil.

With regard to physical evil, it seems that an independent discussion of it in the light of this theory would be lengthy and inconclusive; I therefore include it only in so far as it is necessarily connected with moral evil. For the rest, I merely state my impression that all physical evil could be included, and that the mere unity and universality of a good theory would be a strong initial argument in favour of doing so.

In the moral field I proceed as follows, keeping so far as possible to the philosophical level. The highest finite good is that of the free creature explicitly or implicitly choosing God with his own free will. At the natural level, no other created value can for a moment compare with this. Free will is a reflection, an oblique participation, of God's *aseitas*, that by which God is the reason of His own existence. The free creature can never be the reason of its own existence, but it can, under God, be the reason of its own goodness and its own eternal destiny. It is suggested that for the height of meritorious free choice it is not sufficient that the will should passively accept God, as it would if God made Himself overwhelmingly attractive to the will; but it is necessary that the will should choose God in the face of objective difficulty overcome out of love of God. Only opposition can elicit the height of love, because it elicits the height of *self*-determination, the bracing of the self to win through to what it has chosen to love in spite of all odds. More than that, serious objective difficulty must be present from the nature of the situation. I mean that the free creature, from the nature of the situation, has to choose and love a God he can know only indirectly. This is true of man, of the angels in their state of trial, and of any possible free creature that has not been granted the Beatific Vision. Such is the natural situation, a challenge involving inherent difficulty, and proportionate risk of failure and splendour in achievement. If this is so it immediately requires the existence of physical evil in the life of a free creature; the difficulty in question is physical evil by definition because it is not moral evil. Note that this is not to say that subjective difficulty is the measure of merit: a false doctrine. Love is the measure of merit, but it is suggested that the height of love cannot be elicited otherwise than through objective difficulty overcome. The saints, at the end of their lives, had more love, more merit, and in some ways at least less subjective difficulty; though often enough God makes fresh demands on them in proportion to their hard-won strength. But their later strength, their comparative freedom from subjective difficulty, is won by a lifetime of effort to overcome what was at first comparatively difficult not only objectively but also subjectively. This natural situation may easily be allowed to absorb and include the lesser physical difficulties as well as stress of soul.

In a world in which free creatures have the opportunity of developing the highest love in the face of difficulty, the risk and natural likelihood of failure become proportionately great. It may be morally impossible, and on ultimate analysis metaphysically impossible, that is, absolutely impossible, because involving a contradiction in God, that there should be a whole world of free creatures without any moral failure anywhere. Here the obvious question presents itself: cannot a God of infinite power, who can ensure moral good, as has been allowed, wherever He chooses, without detriment to created freedom, ensure that there should be nothing but moral good everywhere and in all cases? St Augustine dismisses the question with a brief 'God forbid that we should say that God cannot prevent evil'; and theologically we have the proposition of Abelard condemned in 1140 by the Council of Sens: *Quod Deus nec debeat nec possit mala impedire*—that God neither should nor can prevent evils. Further, there is the certain fact that, among purely human creatures, the Blessed Virgin was preserved from all sin whatsoever. In reply one may suggest that God certainly can prevent evil, moral and physical, in particular cases, by ordinary or special providence. What is not so clear is that particular cases can be generalized so as to give the proposition: 'God can prevent physical and moral evil in a whole world of free creatures in all cases whatsoever.' There might well be a contradiction in saying that God created natures of a certain kind, and then, by universal miracle, prevented them from acting according to their natures. To make exceptions in particular cases is intelligible; to make exceptions universal seems to be a contradiction in terms. St Thomas appears to acknowledge this principle when he says:

> . . . it does not belong to divine providence to exclude entirely from things the possibility of failing in good. But this possibility of failing issues in evil of some kind, *because what can fail, sometimes does fail*. Further, the chief characteristic of any good direction is to provide for the things directed in accordance with their natures. . . . Thus, just as it would be out of keeping with right human government to hinder men from acting according to the offices they hold, except perhaps for a short time in some case of necessity, in the same way it would be out of keeping with divine government *not to allow things to act according to their natures*.[1]

And to those who would object that it would have been better not to have created the natures at all, he has many good reasons to offer to the contrary, one of which is that in that case the good in the universe would be not increased but decreased.[2]

---

[1] *Contra Gentiles*, 3:71.

[2] This chapter of the *Contra Gentiles* (3:71) contains an admirable summary of St Thomas's principles in the matter. Those not acquainted with his mind might be puzzled by a sort of blandness or happy unconcern about the problem of evil, and an impression that he seems to find an almost embarrassing number of good reasons for God's permission of evil. The reasons jostle and interpenetrate, and he does not bother to sort them out or elaborate them much. St Thomas's stance here as elsewhere is dictated by his sound method. He has not the slightest doubt about the solution of the problem: the solution is God; and he knows perfectly well that we cannot see the solution as God sees it,

It might be objected, again, that the physical possibility of failure is not necessary for merit, from the theological consideration that Christ as a divine Person had no physical possibility of moral failure yet merited in His human nature. To this it may be replied that what is true of a divine Person who has assumed a human nature is not to be simply transferred to a human person's human nature. The essential for merit is love: the essential for the height of merit, it is suggested, is objective difficulty faced and overcome out of love; and this Christ had in His human nature from the first, because of His foreknowledge of His whole life and death. What seems certain is that without moral failure a large part of the virtues, and perhaps the better part of them, perhaps more than half the ultimate good in the universe, would vanish. There could have been no Christ *as He was*, and no Mother of Christ *as she was*, without the sins of men.

The theory is commended, as Fr Rickaby points out, by the fact that there are no known exceptions to it. The angels are no exception. It is not reasonable to suppose that some of them failed unless their trial was objectively severe. Our first parents are no exception although, as has been said, they had everything in their favour, naturally and supernaturally. The saints are no exception: not one of them but practised heroic virtue in the face of grave objective difficulty. Children dying before the use of reason are no

---

because we cannot see God. That is why, in giving his copious store of reasons, he can afford to be optimistic. He knows his reasons cannot amount to vision, but he is confident that they are well founded, that they point in the right direction; so that he can afford to neglect what, to the man who is still seeking God, would be a serious difficulty—the fact that the principles one can give may be very sound, but seem less so when one looks around the world and tries to assess with a finite mind their application by an infinite mind.

exception if it be granted that theirs is not the uniquely excellent achievement of the free choice of God in the face of difficulty. Not having the use of freedom, they are not human in the fullest sense; yet their inclusion in the good of the universe adds to its beauty a type of innocence which is a partial reflection of the innocence of the supreme creature, the humanity of Christ. God could produce this type of good, and the universe is the better for its inclusion. The Mother of Christ is no exception because her merits were won the hardest way, by her love of God in the face of the sins of men who assailed her through Christ, her Son and her God. Christ Himself is no exception, but rather the supreme exemplar of creaturehood.

The whole plan of creation is good if evil is adequately compensated by resultant good; and, to look no further, the merits of Christ, in virtue of His being a divine Person, have a dimension which makes them incommensurable with any other created or creatable good. Finally, it does not seem that there is anything in any source of Christian doctrine that would exclude the theory, which is here commended to the sympathetic attention of philosophers and theologians.

PART THREE

THE EXISTENCE OF GOD

7

Invalid Reasons for Holding the Existence of God

1. *Introductory*

IF, as the Christian claims, God exists, and if 'God made me to know Him, love Him, and serve Him in this world, and to be happy with Him for ever in the next', the question arises, what provision has God made for men to find Him? In the light of what has been said in Part One of this essay on the relation between reason and revelation, it will not surprise the reader to learn that for the Catholic the answer will be contained, before all else, in one word: the Church. Men are invited to find and recognize Christ, God and man, living in His Church, and in Him to find an answer to all their questions about God, to find a God they can love and serve, and the supernatural strength enabling them to do so. But those who do not accept the Catholic faith may also find God. Sometimes it will be through accepting some version of Christian revelation through some non-Catholic tradition. In this case there will often be special emphasis on the religious experience of the individual, to compensate for the comparative lack of evidence and authority embodied in the organization to which they belong. Others may accept God through some non-Christian religion; others again without any special affiliation. Where non-Catholics are concerned,

it will always be possible to ask the question whether it is
really God they are accepting. If a person for any reason
insists that God is, say, finite or impersonal, and makes that
a condition of his acceptance, then he is not accepting God;
though a man could accept God while making a simple
mistake about some point of His nature. One would hardly
expect to find a non-Christian who called himself a Thomist
philosopher; yet it may well be that many hold the existence
of God for reasons which are at least implicitly the same as
those offered by St Thomas: from the need of a personal first
cause of the existence and order of the world. In practice,
then, it will not be far from the mark to say that the reasons
offered by St Thomas for holding the existence of God are a
possible analysis of what the Christian holds to be true—an
explicit drawing out of the way his mind can work and
probably does work, concomitantly with his acceptance of
Christ's revelation—rather than an analysis of a way he
walked in arriving at the existence of God independently of
revelation. Occasionally one hears of people today who were
helped to certainty about God by such reasons as St Thomas
gives, but by that time they were usually on the threshold of
Christianity. And yet much of what St Thomas says in his
reasons for holding the existence of God may be found in
pagan philosophers.

   Still, it must be emphasized that, whatever people may
say, however imperfectly they may be able to analyse their
own states of mind, there are objectively valid and invalid
reasons for holding the existence of God. The Thomist
claims that, in the sphere of reason, the famous Five Ways
of St Thomas are, in a general way and properly interpreted, valid ways, without thereby saying there are not
other valid ones; but he does say there are some invalid
ones. I wish to begin by examining certain approaches to

God which may be called, broadly, intuitive; which invite a man to see or to feel, rather than to argue or conclude. This will be all the more necessary since much recent work in natural theology has claimed to be both intuitive and Thomist.

2. *The Ontological Argument*

I begin at the metaphysical end of the territory by examining that orchid in the garden of errors, the Ontological Argument,[1] which defends not direct intuition of God but the view that the existence of God can be shown simply by analysis of the idea or notion of God. To understand this famous argument thoroughly is one way of seeing that intuition of God in the sense of direct vision of God is impossible in this life.

The argument has several forms, the first chronologically being that associated with the name of St Anselm (d. 1109), who proposed it in his *Proslogium*. It may be doubted, however, whether Anselm considered it simply a showing of the existence of God and not rather a confirmation or suggestive line of thought, insufficient by itself. Anselm's formulation may be expressed as follows: 'God is rightly conceived as a being than which a greater cannot be thought. But a being who exists in the actual order and not merely as an object of thought is greater than a being who exists merely in the order of thought, i.e. simply, God exists.' This argument on first hearing usually provokes at least a smile. We naturally protest, 'A being, even an infinite being, who is thought of as existing, does not thereby exist.' This is a true refutation.

---

[1] The name Ontological Argument originated about the time of Kant, and indicates that the argument attempts to derive existence (τὸ ὄν) from the logical order, the order of concepts or thoughts.

The argument is false in all its forms—in that of Anselm, and in the later forms given by Descartes (d. 1650) and by Leibniz (d. 1716), which will be examined presently.

All those who reject the argument hold that it makes an unwarranted step from the logical order to the real order, that is, from the order of mere thought to the order of actuality; and this is the ground of St Thomas's refutation in the *Summa Theologica*, 1:2:1, and in the *Contra Gentiles*, 1:10 and 11, and also of Kant's, though not everything that Kant says in the course of his refutation can be accepted.

Every form of the argument may be refuted as follows: the existence of God is not shown by the Ontological Argument, because from the mere notion of God it cannot be certain that God is possible.

Evidently if we cannot be certain that God is possible, we cannot be certain that He exists. The notion of God in question is that of infinite being or any true equivalent. And the refutation amounts to this, that the mere notion of infinite being, though it cannot be shown to have any internal contradiction, at the same time cannot be shown to be free from internal contradiction: there may be an internal contradiction that we cannot detect. (How, then, it may be asked, do we ever know that God, infinite being, is possible? We know this indirectly by showing that God exists and cannot be finite; and that God exists is known not by examining the mere notion of God but by starting with the existence of the world.)

Enough has been said about analogical knowledge to show why the above refutation is true. Our concept of God indicates God, distinguishes Him from finite things, and, in its own imperfect, indirect way, tells us something about His nature. But the imperfection of the analogical way of knowledge does not allow us to penetrate to the nature of

God as it is in itself; and this is readily confirmed by the difficulties which multiply in proportion as the notion of God is evolved. The difficulties are never decisive: it cannot be shown that they create impossibilities; but we cannot see the answers to the difficulties that are manufactured by the fact that our minds are finite and have to think of God analogically. How is God at once absolutely necessary and free? How can God permit evil? How can He be absolutely simple, and yet know finite things in full detail?—and so on. A decisive confirmation is to be found in revelation. If, in our analysis of the notion of God, we arrived at the conclusion that God is three Persons—and it is already significant that we never do arrive at this conclusion, though it is essential to God—we should be obliged to say, 'I cannot actually see that such a thing is impossible, but at the same time I cannot at all see how it is possible.' So far as we are concerned in this life, the Blessed Trinity is a mystery essentially impenetrable to the human mind. In this life we believe it; in the next life we shall know it.

The question is sometimes raised whether, if the possibility of God were evident from the mere notion of God, the step from the order of possibility to that of actuality would be legitimate; but the question is an unreal one. Since God's essence is absolutely identical with His existence, to know His essence directly would be to know His existence directly; there could be no question of a step from the one to the other.

'God exists' may be said to be, in a sense, immediately evident in itself; but it is not immediately evident to us. The sense in which it is immediately evident in itself is that in which God exists and is immediately evident and intelligible to Himself; but 'God exists' is not immediately evident to us, but indirectly evident, that is, by starting with the existence of the world and reasoning from that.

The above conclusion may now be applied to the Onto-logical Argument in its three chief forms:

(1) The form given by Anselm may be expressed as beginning with the statement that 'God *is* the Being than which a greater cannot be thought'. That God is so conceived may be granted; that God as thus defined exists may be denied until His existence is proved some other way. 'That which exists in the real order is greater than that which exists in the order of mere possibility.' This statement begs the question. There can be no question of existence in the real order unless the being in question is possible; and it has not yet been shown that 'a being than which a greater cannot be thought' is possible and not self-contradictory.

(2) The form defended by Descartes may be expressed as follows: 'What is contained in the clear and distinct idea of a thing must be affirmed of the thing; but existence is contained in the clear and distinct idea of God, for His essence is identical with His existence; therefore existence must be affirmed of God, i.e. God exists.' What is contained in the clear and distinct idea of a thing is to be affirmed of the *idea* of the thing, but not of the *thing* unless you know that the thing exists; and here you do not even know that the thing *can* exist. Your clear and distinct idea is not clear and distinct at all. Descartes has set up the hypothesis of a being whose essence is identical with existence, but this does not amount to a clear and distinct idea; and the suggested identity of essence and existence may turn out on closer inspection to be an impossible notion, a mirage. It does not do so in fact, but neither on the other hand does it ever become clear, from the mere inspection of the idea, that such a thing is positively possible.

(3) The form defended by Leibniz may be expressed as follows: 'If God is possible, He exists; but God is possible;

therefore He exists.' In reply it can be said that from the mere notion of God, God is *negatively* possible, that is, we cannot see that He is impossible; but not *positively* possible, that is, we cannot tell whether or not there is a latent impossibility.

'If God is possible He exists.' This is perfectly true. For if God were possible and yet did not exist, this would involve a contradiction: God, as identical with existence, *could not* be non-existent; as merely possible, He *could* be non-existent.

Nevertheless there is a tendency, strong in some types of mind, to think that we can see the possibility of infinite being by simply considering the notion. If the refutation given above is correct, this is an error; and it will be worth while to try to track it to its sources by considering some further difficulties.

(1) In the account of analogical knowledge it was stated that our concept of God is 'very inadequate', and represents God only imperfectly. *But*, the objection might run, *if that is so, we must have somehow an adequate and perfect knowledge of God, by comparison with which we realize that our concept of God is inadequate and imperfect*. This difficulty owes its plausibility to a trick of the imagination. We know other examples of inadequate knowledge compared with adequate knowledge in our own experience, and transfer the mental process and pictures to the case in hand, imagining God, perhaps, as an indefinitely extended background, and our apprehension of Him as some sketchy or indirect approach to this; or, being convinced on other grounds that God is simple and definite, we subconsciously allow ourselves to think that He can be as simple and definite in our minds as He is in Himself.

(2) *God's nature is sheer, simple Being: but in the notion of sheer*

*simple Being there can be no possibility of internal contradiction;
for this would imply incompatibility of different and limited elements;
but there can be no different and limited elements in sheer, simple
Being.* This is a good objection. It can be shown that an
infinite being, if it can exist, must also be absolutely simple,
and this seems to exclude the possibility of internal contradiction. However, our name for it, 'absolute simplicity', is
deceptively easy. What does it really amount to? What sort
of grasp do we have of absolute simplicity? Exactly the
same grasp as we have of that from which it is derived,
namely, infinite being: and we do not know from the mere
notion that infinite being is possible. When the easy-
sounding notion of absolute simplicity is in turn evolved, it
turns out to be full of difficulties. And, as I have mentioned,
we learn from revelation that absolute simplicity is threeness of Persons, something whose possibility we cannot see
but can only believe. So the objector has been deceived by
the sound of words. Absolute simplicity is not apprehended
as absolutely simple. It is indicated by a complex concept
made up of three notes, viz. 'being', 'not', and 'finite'; and
one cannot see, merely by examining the notion, that
'being' and 'infinite' are compatible.

(3) This leads to a third objection based on two meanings of infinite. The objection might run: *It is clear from the
mere consideration of the idea that the infinite is possible; because
we can always think of further and greater being beyond any assignable limit; and what is thinkable is possible.* The first answer is
very simple: we can think of further and greater being
beyond any assignable limit. But the question is, can we
think of further and greater being *infinitely* beyond any
assignable limit? It is true that we can go on indefinitely
thinking further and greater possibility, but it is not clear
that we can by that process leave the region of finite

possibility. The 'indefinitely expanding' infinite does not approach the absolute infinite; it never begins to approach it; the absolute infinite transcends it and all its indefinite possibility. Is it clear that absolute infinity is possible, simply from examining the notion? The answer must be that it is not. One can use the form of words, 'absolute, transcendent infinite', and allow oneself to be tricked by the imagination into thinking it is directly intelligible, but there is every reason to think that this is a mistake; it is the result of the scaling-down process to which our minds are naturally prone.

The same objection may be expressed this way: *Can we, yes or no, assign limits to our thought?* The disjunction is not complete. In simply considering the notion of absolute infinity there is a third possibility, namely, I don't know; and this, understood in the sense of the last paragraph, is, I think, the right reply.

It is sometimes thought that divergence on this point indicates two radically opposed metaphysical outlooks, splitting the scholastic world from top to bottom. It may be doubted whether this is so, and whether the true causes are not rather certain psychological pressures. There are several such at work. I have mentioned the trick of the imagination by which a scaled-down image of transcendence is applied to the transcendence of God. There is the further one, that all scholastic philosophers know that God, the transcendent infinite, is in fact possible; so that it becomes easy to forget the process by which this knowledge is arrived at philosophically. The mind which tries to see the possibility of infinite being by the frontal attack is the same mind that can come to see that possibility by a psychologically slight but philosophically all-important turn of thought, by which it is possible to conclude, and, before concluding, to feel the pressure of the process by which we can conclude, that if finite being exists, then infinite being exists as its only sufficient reason.

I cannot, therefore, accept the position of those scholastic philosophers who hold that infinite being is part of the meaning of finite being, or that finite being cannot be understood except by reference to infinite being, in the ordinary acceptance of the words used. The point will arise again when St Thomas's Fourth Way comes up for discussion. There it will be necessary to examine the significance of saying that finite being is possible beyond the range of the existing finite being of our experience.

While acknowledging that the Platonic or Augustinian line of thought has its value and, far from being eternally opposed to the Aristotelean, rather converges towards it, I do not think it is sufficient by itself, and I do not think St Thomas thought that it was.

(3) *Ontologism*

Proceeding one stage nearer to direct awareness of God as understood by what is called religious experience, a word may here be said about Ontologism. This is not a doctrine of awareness of God in the feelings or by any kind of special religious sense, but claims that either all knowledge (including sense knowledge), or at least intellectual knowledge as such, is 'vision in God' in the sense that, in knowing, we have as the direct object of our minds, not the very essence of God, but—an impossible distinction made by Ontologists —some aspect or part of God: God *qua* creator, or the ideas in the divine mind.

It cannot be said that Ontologism is today the live issue it was in the middle of the last century when for decades it

rocked the boat of scholasticism; but every error is instructive, and almost every error about God has, or may easily
come to have, its contemporary counterpart.

There is in our minds, when we know, nothing that
allows us to say either, 'This is obviously God, I recognize
Him immediately', or, 'I did not realize it at first, but now I
come to think it out, this item of my thought must certainly
involve direct vision of the mind of God'. Note that it is not
a question of the *effects* of God in our knowledge or experience internal or external. Obviously it may be concluded
that we know the effects of God in the world and in our
minds and feelings, because in fact everything, in so far as it
is, is a direct effect of God. What is meant is that we have
no immediate intuition of God Himself in or with the
effects He produces in the world. If we conclude that it is
God who produces the effects, it must be a conclusion and
not direct vision of God.

The question concerns only normal human experience.
Whether the saints in mystical contemplation are ever
granted any kind of direct vision of God is another matter.
If they are, and if it amounts to the Beatific Vision, then it is
supernatural and miraculous.

The name Ontologism was coined by Gioberti, an Italian
Ontologist, in the middle of the last century to indicate the
view that reality and our knowledge of it go hand in hand to
such an extent that God, the first reality, must also be the
first reality we know. In spite of the similarity of name there
is no very close similarity with the Ontological Argument.

The view that human thought keeps pace with reality so
that the more intelligible a thing is in itself, the more
intelligible it is to us, is often said to be a Platonic way of
thinking, and there is a good deal of truth in this. For Plato,
the objects of our thoughts are the Forms, entities existing

in their own right in a separate world of their own; and the
mind in thinking sees these entities directly. If this world of
Forms is transferred to the mind of God, as it was by
Plotinus and St Augustine, it would be an easy step, but a
false one, to say that when we think, we have direct insight
into the mind of God Himself.

In modern philosophy, a fresh approach to the same
faulty conclusion was prepared for by the theory of Descartes that soul and body are radically separate, with no
bridge between sense and intellect; so that the thoughts we
have about things are not caused by things, but arise in our
minds on the occasion of seeing things. The doctrine of
Occasionalism defended by Malebranche (d. 1715) and
others, claimed that ideas in our minds can be caused by
God alone. Malebranche himself went further and held that
what happens when we think, or even when we see, is that
we are simply looking directly into the mind of God. This is
Ontologism in its extreme form, the view that we see even
individual material things, and know everything, 'in the
mind of God', in the sense that we see in the divine mind the
pattern-ideas by reference to which God creates the world.
Similarly Gioberti (d. 1852) held that we know all things
'in God' in the sense that we know God directly in His
creative act, and not merely the effects of it. In the middle
of the nineteenth century a strong school of Ontologists
restricted their theory to intellectual knowledge, but allowed
that we have sense knowledge of trees and tables simply by
looking at them. Finally, Rosmini (d. 1855) held cognate
views which were formulated for condemnation by a decree
of the Holy Office in words which may be translated thus:
'Existence, thought of indeterminately, without specifying
whether it is the existence of God or of creatures, is something divine'; 'The existence of which man has an intuition

must necessarily be an element of eternal and necessary being; . . . but this is God'. Several similar formulae may be found, with the above, in Denzinger, *Enchiridion*, (ed. 14–15) n. 1891 sq.; but there is room for doubt whether the condemned formulae fairly represent Rosmini's real view.

The Ontologist theory may be refuted as follows: No part of our mental experience is recognizable, either before or after reflection or argument, as immediate intuition of God; more than that, reflection and argument from sound principles exclude the view that any part of our mental experience is thus recognizable.

In the above statement, the qualifying word 'recognizable' is inserted so as not to exclude a view that is different from Ontologism, is thought by some to be a possible view, and is not unorthodox theologically.[1]

All Ontologists appeal to something recognizable in mental experience, and invite us to agree that it must be God. Most of the nineteenth century Ontologists appealed specially to what are called necessary truths like those of mathematics and metaphysics. A truth like $2 + 2 = 4$ is, they urged, eternally and necessarily true; but what is eternal and necessary is God; therefore these truths are part of God. The conclusion does not follow. Such necessary truths are obtained by observing finite things and thinking away the particularity of what is observed, i.e. by abstraction: not this 2 and this 2 equal this four, but any possible pair of two's equal four. The 'necessity' and 'eternity' which such truths possess are not the necessity and eternity of God, but something essentially lower which is found in finite things and is, in the last analysis, part of their meaning. But this finite necessity is not absolute in every way. $2 + 2 = 4$ is true of any possible pair of 2's; but it is not absolutely necessary

[1] See the *Note* at the end of the section.

that there should be any 2's for it to be true about, or any
finite minds to know them. God's necessity, by contrast, is
absolute in every way. The fact of some kind of necessity
does not immediately indicate God. Even what is called a
'mere fact' has some necessity about it, something absolute.
A mere fact must be what it is, and not something else at
the same time and in the same respect. This minimal
necessity and absoluteness belongs to every thing as what
it is and part of its meaning; it cannot be denied without
re-affirming it in the denial. If this is true of concrete facts,
it will be true in a new way of immaterial facts and principles of thought. Two stones may become three stones by
division, but twoness cannot become threeness. Again, the
'eternity' of such principles is not the eternity of God; it
merely abstracts from time, just as it abstracts from place,
in virtue of being immaterial in our immaterial minds. St
Thomas concludes: 'It does not follow that these things are
eternal except as they exist in an eternal mind—if there is
one.'[1]

The contention that we see the 'necessary truths' of
mathematics and metaphysics in the mind of God is wholly
gratuitous. The explanation that attributes these truths, as
they exist in our minds, to the mind's abstractive power is
quite satisfactory. How they do in fact exist in the mind of
God is a question whose answer is not to us sufficiently clear
to be very relevant. For St Thomas, their truth as it exists
in God is inseparable from His infinite essence: 'We do not
see the truth of things (*rationes rerum*: strictly, creatable
things as they exist in God's thought) as it exists in God: to
do so would necessarily involve seeing the essence of God.'[2]

What exactly Rosmini meant by an intuition of 'exist-

[1] *Summa Theologica*, 1:16:7 in the reply to objection 2.
[2] *De Spiritualibus Creaturis* 10 in the reply to objection 8.

ence in general' is not a question to embark on here. But on
the showing of the formulae attributed to him, 'existence in
general' cannot be specifically divine, because it is equally
verified in creatures. Similarly, our idea of 'being in
general', however it is conceived, is not specifically divine
because it includes creatures; and in any case our idea of
God is no intuition of God, but is obtained by negation of
finiteness.

Our experience of ourselves might give rise to error in the
matter. The saturation of the self through mind and sense
that can be produced by contemplation of nature, or
through artistic contemplation, or through love, can cul-
minate in a condition whose description is in many ways
close to that given by the great mystics of their highest
states of contemplation of God—a darkness and blankness
that is more than light and thought. But there need be no
confusion. The apparent condition and its description are
not the only factors involved. The saturation is that of the
human person at certain levels, in part observable and
describable; the objects towards which the mind and will
are directed in its production are a different matter altogether; they may be as different as finite and infinite. For
the artist, the experience may be accepted for its own sake,
or may point beyond itself to he knows not what; the mystic
for his part, knows very well the difference between contemplating God and contemplating any other object.

Finally, the sense of dependence on God which some may
claim to have is no intuition of God, but a reminder-feeling
accompanying knowledge otherwise acquired that we
depend on God. The same may be said, for similar reasons,
of the working of the moral conscience.

That God cannot be known directly and clearly by
finite minds in this life follows immediately from St

Thomas's theory of knowledge. In direct knowledge, the knower acquires a perfection equal to that of the object known, so far as it is known. But a finite intellect has no natural capacity to receive the perfection of infinite being. God, therefore, cannot be known directly, but only indirectly, analogically. In the Beatific Vision, a finite intellect by a finite act knows God directly but not comprehensively. For St Thomas this is a mystery in the strict sense and one of the supreme examples of divine power. If a share in it is ever given to the saints in this life, this too is supernatural and miraculous, and no part of normal human knowledge.

Note on the possibility of an 'obscure' intuition of God. Some philosophers, e.g., Gabriel Picard, S.J. in *La saisie immédiate de Dieu dans les états mystiques* (1923) would defend the possibility of an *obscure* intuition of God in this life, even at the level of nature and apart from the mystical experience which can be the culmination of the life of grace. This would not be Ontologism, as will be clear from the definitions. An obscure intuition is one whose object is not distinguishable from other objects, even after reflection and attention; it is not nameable with certainty and has no intelligible content of its own; it never makes it possible to say, 'This is God', or even 'This must be God', but only 'This may be God'. This kind of intuition is described as a feeling or a touch, not as an intelligible object of knowledge; it never becomes clear-confused, distinguishable from other objects, even under reflection, but remains subconscious or even unconscious. There is nothing contradictory about such a notion. It is possible to have an experience that is so dim that we can never be sure what it is; or one that we are not aware of at all—but we should be aware of the difference if it were removed.

The advantages of the theory are that it provides a natural point of insertion for supernatural mystical states without necessarily impairing their supernatural character; and provides an explanation for the apparent specialness and sense of immediacy that can accompany the exercise of mind and will about God even in ordinary prayer. However, the theory is not easy to defend philosophically, and it is very doubtful whether St Thomas, to whom appeal is made by Picard, really meant that. More probably all the appearances could be saved by saying that the most that is ever given at the level of nature and even at the level of ordinary graces is not any kind of intuition of God Himself but only of the effects of God in the soul. God is unique, and it is not surprising if the mind and will exercised about God should be accompanied by unique feelings, especially when closely united to God. So much may suffice in the context of Ontologism. More will be said about mystical experience in the following section.

4. *Religious experience: Fideism and Modernism*

But people quite often do claim to have direct awareness of God in this life, so what is happening? Briefly I would say that, with a possible exception to be specified presently, they are mistaking awareness of the effects of God in the soul for awareness of God Himself; mistaking part of the evidence for the existence of God for the whole of it. Their experience is not by itself able to give them more than subjective assurance; it cannot stand up to objective criticism if it claims to be direct awareness of God, so as to be adequate evidence for His existence.

Religious experience is a phrase of many meanings. The Thomist approaches the problem of sorting them out from the point of view of the nature of God and of man and man's relations to God. His conclusion is that man has intellect and will and senses, the last including all the bodily feelings; and that, apart from mystical experience in the

strict sense, he has no specifically religious way of knowing
and no direct awareness of God either through intellectual
intuition or through the feelings or through both. He may
indeed have unique feelings associated with his knowledge
and love of God, but in ordinary cases that does not imply
a unique religious sense or a special religious way of knowing. Man's relation to God is that of a creature whose first
duty is to know God, to love and worship Him, and to be
ready to do all God's will in his regard so far as this is made
known to him, and thus to achieve his final end with God
in the next life. He has a mind to know God, a will to love
Him, and feelings which may either greatly help or greatly
hinder mind and will. Evidently the exercise of any or all of
these—mind, will, feelings—in relation to God may be
called religious experience in a wide sense. Further, these
items of human equipment, though they are distinct, are
not and cannot be kept in separate compartments; they
form the unity that is man, and they are all operative to a
greater or lesser extent in every human act concerned with
God or with anything else. In their normal working the
three factors are closely combined, and any attempt to
separate them by analysing a concrete human act or experience tends to involve some loss, which is one of the draw-
backs of philosophy. If a person prefers not to analyse
a human experience, or finds on doing so that it seems to
have been torn apart and all the life taken out of it, he may
leave it unanalysed and call it simply a feeling or an
experience.

Here the parallel with the working of the moral conscience is instructive. A person may say, and some philosophers do say, that to keep a promise is right and to break
a promise is wrong, and that they just 'see' this as something
as simple as seeing yellow and blue; that it does not need to

be analysed or otherwise justified, and is not capable of being. Such people are perfectly right in saying it is evidently right to keep a promise, and that, as items of experience, these obvious obligations do normally confront one as simple pressures or imperatives of a unique sort called moral. But if some philosophers see moral obligation as something irreducible and unanalysable, it does not follow that it is unanalysable by others who see differently the nature of the factors involved and the principles applicable to the task of analysis. When this happens, both parties will be talking about exactly the same experience, but describing it in different terms. The Thomist holds that moral obligation in general, and particular obligations, can be analysed and philosophically speaking need to be; and that the same is true of religious experience. Moreover, he holds that the feeling part strictly so called, the part of the senses, imagination, interior feelings of pleasure and pain, attraction and repulsion, is a very tricky thing indeed, and that to regard it as in all cases self-justifying is to be heading for trouble theoretical and practical; that these feelings and their fruits are subject to the judgment of reason and, it may be, of God's authority, and that ultimately nothing else can justify them; though, to be sure, at the practical level reason *may* be at work, and working correctly, even if its working is not analysed. But if a person refuses to reflect on his experiences in this human way, he cannot justify his conclusions from them to himself or to others; he can only say 'I have a feeling'; but what the cause or objective content of the feeling is, he is powerless to say. Rejection of these principles enables people to talk seriously about 'Religion without God', and to say 'The question, Is religion true? has no meaning.' Even those who, so far as words go, speak of God and claim to be in touch with Him, cannot justify their position so long as they confine themselves to subjective experience alone.

This attitude, which may be called broadly Fideism, the Thomist sees as involving a serious mistake of method, a mistake of emphasis springing in some cases from a fundamental divergence of principles. For the Thomist, religious truth, whether it is a conclusion of reason or a revealed truth, can be expressed in a formula which is objectively true and whose object may be outside our present experience. What we feel about it subjectively, the difference it makes to our happiness in the various circumstances of life, is a consequence of this truth, and not the truth itself, and not its ultimate test and justification. This makes the Catholic's outlook largely other-worldly, though he realizes as well as anyone that his lot in the next life depends on his behaviour in this, and that he has obligations to his fellow men as well as to God. For those who doubt or deny the capacity of the human mind to transcend experience in this way, who, though they want to hold the existence of God in some sense, find themselves agnostic about His nature and about a future life, the experience of this life becomes not secondary and derivative but primary and perhaps ultimate. For them the mind's capacity for truth must be satisfied here and now; if anything exists outside the experience of this life, they are content to know very little about it and hope for the best. They tend, therefore, to say that God simply *is* what we experience in this life in our highest aspirations; and that whatever else He is or may be cannot much matter to us. This is the wrong emphasis which the Thomist regards as a fundamental mistake. It consists in putting not God but man in the centre of the picture, in making God's essential role to satisfy and enrich men here and now. The certainty which the Catholic attains about

God produces in the depths of his soul a tranquillity which cannot be conveyed to those who have not known it; but he does not mistake this experience for God. For the Fideist the situation is quite different. He says:

> No: there is, indeed, nothing to compare with the truth. But truth requires that we should admit the limitations of our knowledge. We know what we experience. Our experience contains and suggests to us values greater than ourselves: let us call them God. We have a feeling of dependence: on what? Let us call it God. Our experience enables us to postulate something which allows man to go ahead exercising his spiritual powers in the world without feeling overwhelmed by the world; because he thinks there is a power on which the world depends, which is ruling the world for spiritual ends.

But what if these feelings are not God? What if their explanation does not require God? How will he know that God exists? Ineffable, numinous, awe-inspiring, *mysterium tremendum*, absolute Being, God, all are but words and their objects mere finite human thoughts and experiences unless it can be shown that there *is* a transcendent Being who is infinite and personal, the first beginning and the last end of the world.

Fideism can justify itself before reason only by running with the hare and hunting with the hounds, as Schleiermacher did in describing religion as a feeling of dependence on the infinite. Either there is dependence on an infinite personal God or there is not. If there is, more is involved than mere feeling; if there is not, there is no religious experience. The only alternative to the infinite is the finite. No infinity, no God; no God, no religion.

To apply these principles to the religions of the world, and in particular to the religious experience of the various Christian bodies, would be too long a task to embark on here. It must suffice to say that so far as such experiences are good and true they are the work of God; so far as they fall short of goodness and truth as willed by God for men and for these men, they are the work of man. But God's kindly light leads men by various ways. Men are not always aware how good God is being to them; and in the depths of their souls they may have more knowledge and love of God than they can put into words; and words may positively betray them if they attempt the task.

The following application of Thomist principles may be suggested as an elementary sketch of an explanation of what is happening in the ordinary run of cases when people claim to have direct awareness of God. Such states may be explained as an alignment or interpenetration of intellect in three of its functions: (i) immediate concomitant awareness of the self in all knowledge; (ii) quasi-intuition of the self as enriched by knowledge; (iii) analogical knowledge of God.

The human person, while it is never intuitive of itself in the full sense of intellectual intuition, can, by the ordinary co-operation and interplay of sense and intellect, be enriched to a kind of saturation which may be described as quasi-intuition of the finite objects contemplated, and of the self. The occasion of the enrichment, the objects contemplated, may be something in the realm of art or of nature or of human persons; or it may be God—but this last in a special way, as will be said presently. What is enriched is the human person in some department, at some level; but by a kind of resonance, the experience at one level may awaken echoes at all levels, and point beyond itself to all possible experience, and to God. The description of these states, occasioned as they are by different objects, may be superficially very similar: stillness, saturation, satisfaction, darkness rather than light, the apparent transcending of definiteness and distinction, more than can be put into words. If the occasion is music, say, or nature, this may remind one of, or arouse by resonance, love of people in general, or of a particular person, or of God. People may, however, close their ears to the resonance and live for beauty. But this would spoil the perspective, and sooner or later they would be disappointed and agree with Mr Somerset Maugham that beauty is a bit of a bore.

When the object of contemplation is God, a new factor has to be taken into account, or rather re-emphasized, namely the will. If there is not true love of God there cannot be more than what may be called appreciation of God. In this case a man might imagine that he is loving God when really he is only loving music or nature. Yet by resonance there could be aroused the thought of the love of God which he could have if he would. To love God is to have one's will right with God and to renounce all sin and to be ready, implicitly at least, to accept God's will as made known from any source including revelation. This brings the state of sanctifying grace which, though not necessarily an object of experience, affects the soul in ways that can be experienced. When the soul is thus in grace or on the way to it, there can be experiences, especially in prayer, ranging from a passing feeling of consolation to utter absorption in God and unconsciousness of one's surroundings. What is happening in this kind of love of God? Most probably the only object of direct apprehension is the soul as thus enriched in mind and will by the thought of God and love of Him. But the knowing self is directed not to itself but beyond itself to God. And here would be found in the fullest way the interpenetration of quasi-intuition and analogical knowledge. The soul itself would seem to have here a role analogous to that of the phantasm or reminder-image in ordinary knowledge, becoming a reminder or symbol of God who is known to be transcendent. Looking out from itself as thus enriched, the soul knows only blankness, because it cannot directly transcend the finite self. It does not rest in itself, but recognizes as transcendent and answers in love the God who is showing His love of the soul by thus enriching it. This conscious, explicit love of God would therefore be something quite special. No Catholic, certainly no Catholic mystic, would think for a moment of confusing the essentially different states of loving music, loving a human being, and loving God; though in the case of good people the sympathy and interpenetration of the states would enable them to rise rapidly, as did St Teresa of Avila, for example, from contemplating flowers or a river to love of God.

I have spoken so far of circumstances when the person is enriched by experience of the finite. But what is called, rightly or wrongly, natural mysticism is more often associated not with enrichment through the finite but with complete renunciation; with a stripping from oneself of knowledge and love of finite things. Still if such a condition is not to be purely negative, it must be indirectly an enrichment. It may or may not be felt so at first; but those who practise it would not do so if they did not think it so, and find it so at last. It can be in fact, as East and West testify, a way to a uniquely satisfying human experience. On what is the person concentrating when he is thus detached from earthly things? On God, if his way is a healthy one. What is the experience which accompanies his concentration? I should say, the experience not of God but of the self in contact with God. And the focus of the experienced contact would seem to be the soul's immediate contact with itself; not an intellectual intuition of the essence of the soul, but a pre-conceptual contact at the level of existence, in which the absence of clear intelligible content would be compensated by the immediacy.

In recent years attempts have been made to find a highest common factor of what is called mystical experience as reported by witnesses ancient and modern in both East and West. The attempt is a laudable one in so far as it recalls to the Western mind the ancient value of contemplative wisdom, culminating in contemplation of God. But the similarities on which the 'highest common factor' theory are based are in many ways only superficial, and need to be interpreted not with a happy all-inclusiveness but with great caution, as Fr M. C. D'Arcy has recently pointed out in *The Meeting of Love and Knowledge*. Catholic mystics, for their part, all affirm that their high states of experience of God are inseparable from the grace of God, and that they have no guarantee against self-deception independently of submission to the authority of Christ teaching in His Church.

Grace gives a connaturality with God which issues, in the next life, in the immediate vision of God. To what extent can this capacity be actuated in this life? With grace comes a clearness of knowledge and a corresponding depth of love which will often be accompanied by heightened feelings to produce what may be called, globally, unique experience. But I am inclined to think that ordinary experiences of this kind, those available to all mankind, would not, in this life, require frames of explanation essentially different from those suggested above.[1]

[1] The following are what I take to be the commoner and sounder conclusions of theologians of mysticism in this matter: (i) there is no immediate experience of God by purely natural means, i.e. apart from grace; (ii) in the supernatural life of grace, though non-discursive contemplation of God and of divine things as apprehended by faith is quite common, there is no immediate experience of God in any but the final stages; (iii) mystical experience *may* be given by God as the culmination

To Kantian subjectivism in matters of knowledge, and Fideism, or reliance on experience in matters of religion, *Modernism* adds the notion of the evolution of religious experience, an evolution by which truth can be transformed out of all recognition, so that what seemed true and right to one century or generation can seem false and wrong to another; and this not merely in the field of the more difficult questions of morality like some aspects of punishment, but in the broader conclusions about the nature of God, the content of revelation, and His will for the world and for the individual. Nothing is exempt from this process of evolution; all is made relative to present needs and present feelings. In particular, the systematic working out of a body of doctrine, whether in philosophy or theology, is regarded by the Modernist as a monstrosity. Separate formulae, they admit, may have the virtue of crystallizing the experience of a particular generation; but to draw conclusions from these formulae or from principles of reason, or to regard the formulae themselves as embodying what is simply and always true, is anathema to the Modernist.

Besides the historical factors of the philosophy of Kant and the dissipation of revealed doctrine through the weakening of the idea of a teaching authority, other contributory causes of Modernism are not hard to find. Dogmatic theology and scholastic philosophy have not always guarded

---

of the life of grace, after a preparation of love of God through obedience, self-discipline and prayer; (iv) this mystical experience is 'infused', not 'acquired', i.e. it is not obtainable merely by co-operation with graces available to all, but is given by God if He sees fit—it is an experience that is *in some sense* immediate perception of God, but it remains obscure, and is never the clear intuition of the beatific vision; (v) the grace of God is available to all mankind, and there is no reason to deny, and good reason to allow, that God sometimes gives mystical experience to some who through no fault of their own know nothing of His revelation or of the Church which is the normal source of abundant grace.

successfully against mistakes of method resulting in unreal subtlety, pseudo-profundity, not knowing where to stop. Again, philosophy and theology are not the whole of religion; merely by themselves they are not even the beginning of religion, which is essentially an act of love. It does include the feelings and 'experience' part of the time for everybody, though some may scarcely advert to the fact. When the Church was one in Europe, scholastic philosophers and theologians could take the feeling element for granted because, so far as it was needed, it was common to all. Now the feeling element is as diverse, almost, as the doctrines; certainly different people differ very much about what they declare that they 'feel' to be true. It is all a question of the relation between the two, thought and feeling. Do I feel this way because of what I hold to be true, or do I hold certain things to be true because of what I feel? And need I necessarily feel anything at all about a supernatural truth?

Another factor helping to produce the Modernist state of mind is the strangeness of some parts of revelation, and the temptation even to the religious mind, if it has lost the Catholic notion of supernatural faith, to make a clean sweep and regard it all as purely symbolic. From the first chapter of St Matthew, angels, dreams and all, down to, shall we say, the definition of bodily assumption of the Blessed Virgin, how much easier to regard it all as non-literal; how much harder to remember that when God reveals we must be ready for surprises, and, for the rest, patiently to separate the wheat from the chaff in twenty centuries of Christian thought and practice. The Modernist might go on to ask whether it really makes much difference in practice: do we not all believe in the same God and hold the same things to be good and bad, right and wrong for the world ? Can we not all trust to the same Spirit for guidance in our particular needs, corporate and individual, as they arise ? And need we be surprised if the same Spirit inspires us with different desires in different times and circumstances ? Again, he may urge, does your scholastic philosophy and theology really tell you anything about God ? Is it not only a pious hope that it does ? Do you not follow your feelings in the end ? Whose piety is guided by the subtleties of the philosophers and theologians ? Would you really be surprised and disconcerted if all this cobwebspinning were swept away in the vision of the ineffable ?

Anyone who knows the history of religious thought during the past few centuries can readily understand the state of mind. To the Catholic, learned or simple, it seems a morass. He accepts Christ on His terms, and recognizes Him in the Church ; he holds that God has given men minds with which to know and believe the truth about Him ; and he is disinclined to think that in matters of religion He who on earth taught with authority has now left men to flounder. As a busy man he expects to have his religion definite and businesslike ; and he thinks this is entirely compatible with love of God, even heroic love, which, like love of men or of one's country, is essentially a matter of the will founded on solid convictions, and not on mere sentiment. St Pius X called Modernism 'the synthesis of all the heresies'. A few Catholics fell into Modernism at the beginning of the century. How strange that they could forget the saints. No saint but would have rejected the principles of Modernism, instantly and absolutely.

5. *The Practical Postulates of Kant*

According to Immanuel Kant (1724–1804) the freedom of

the will, the immortality of the soul, and the existence of God cannot be proved by the speculative reason, but are what he calls 'postulates of the practical reason', or necessary assumptions of the moral life. This theory is conditioned by Kant's theory of the speculative reason by which he restricts knowledge to phenomena as presented under the subjective forms of space and time and the subjective categories such as those of substance and causality. In spite of the subjectivity he attributes to the speculative reason, Kant wished to save objectivity in the moral sphere, which he considered more important than the speculative sphere. His immediately relevant description of the moral sphere may be summarized as follows:

(i) Moral obligation is a fact which cannot be denied any more than the fact of sensation can be denied. A moral act is a free act: I cannot act morally without thinking that I act freely, i.e. that I initiate activity and do not merely passively respond to inclinations or attractions. In the sphere of external nature, the sphere of the speculative reason, there is no freedom: all phenomena are ruled by rigid determinism as conditioned by the category of causality. But in the moral sphere it cannot be any merely phenomenal self that acts; it must be the real 'noumenal' self, for it acts freely. Nothing more than this can be said about freedom. We have no insight into the noumenal self or its activity; we can only accept them. Freedom is thus the first postulate of the practical reason.

(ii) Practical reason seeks to attain the unconditioned object of the will, i.e. the highest good, which consists of (*a*) perfect virtue, and (*b*) happiness in proportion to virtue. These two, says Kant, 'are conceived as necessarily united, so that the one cannot be apprehended by the practical reason without the other'. But perfect virtue and proportionate happiness are unattainable in this life. Yet the will is obliged to aim at them. They must therefore be attainable in a future life in which progress to perfect virtue may continue indefinitely, and in which virtue may produce the perfect happiness we necessarily will it to produce. Thus the immortality of the soul is the second postulate of the practical reason.

(iii) The third postulate is the existence of God as the highest original good and the cause of the highest derived good, that is, of the order of virtue and happiness and of the ultimate harmony between them. No rational agent who is part of the world can fulfil this function. We must postulate a cause of nature as a whole, and distinct from it. Such a supreme cause must be in harmony with the moral character of moral agents, and must cause through intellect and will.

Kant's reasons for holding the existence of God may be assessed either from the point of view of their coherence with his doctrine of the speculative reason, or merely on their own merits on the assumption that the practical order, as described by him, gives some sort of information, however qualified, about the real as distinct from the phenomenal world. From the first point of view: (i) Kant states that obligation is imposed simply by the form of law, the law that we should act from duty and not merely from sense-inclination or attraction. But this cannot be the whole account of the matter. Duty is an abstraction: what we have is duties. But on Kant's principles it seems impossible to find for these duties any material content which does not belong to the phenomenal order, the order of appearances, not of things in themselves. (ii) Kant supposes that his categories of the understanding are applicable in the moral sphere to the real order. In the sphere of the speculative reason they were for him mere subjective frames for combining sensations into a formal unity; he does not show that they are anything else when used in the moral sphere; yet he uses them in that sphere to show the existence of God. (iii) What grounds has Kant for holding that good as the object of the moral will, and in particular happiness, is something in the real order? On his own principles good and happiness, so far as we can know them, would seem to belong only to the world of phenomena or appearances.

From the point of view simply of the reasons offered by Kant for his postulates (i) Freedom is necessary for moral action, and Kant's claim that we are conscious of initiating action and not merely mediating it is correct and expressed with some acuteness. At the same time, a great deal more than that can and should be said about freedom by philosophers who do not share Kant's views about the restrictions of the speculative intellect. Kant is quite right in holding that if we try to explain freedom in terms of matter and time and space we are bound to get into inextricable difficulties. But freedom, the causality of spirit, can be described and understood analogically. (ii) The will aims at good in general, it aims at virtue, and it aims at happiness. I think Kant is quite right in claiming that obligation is, at least in many cases, imposed on us peremptorily and without evident connection with the happiness it may produce in ourselves or others. For the Thomist, too, the amount of happiness produced in this world is not the test of all right action. There can be cases when we are obliged *not* to do things which would cause happiness in this world—even cases when we are obliged not to do what would produce greater moral goodness in others. That this situation, for those who can accept it, suggests that the moral order cannot be understood simply in terms of this life, is true. I do not however, think that this proves with certainty that there is a future life in which perfect virtue and proportionate happiness may be obtained. If we suppose that God, the author of the moral order, exists, no doubt it is much easier to hold a future life from considerations arising out of the moral order. But if God is not supposed to exist, the moral order as we experience it might involve frustration, or might be explained otherwise. Those who, unlike Kant, do not hold God's existence, may plausibly enough interpret duty simply in terms of happiness in this life, and claim that obligations which have no reference to happiness in this world are illusory. (iii) Granted Kant's first two postulates, the existence of God follows readily enough. If, as Kant says, the object of our will is possible, and if it is not possible in this life, and if neither man himself nor any other part of nature is capable of ensuring that virtue and happiness are combined in a future life, then we must postulate God who is not part of nature, who causes by intelligence and will, and who is the original Good, the cause of all derived good. Kant admits further that the idea of God which is the ideal of the speculative reason—'necessity, infinity, unity, existence apart from the world (not as a soul of the world), eternity as free from conditions of time, omnipresence as unaffected by conditions of space, etc.'—may be applied to the notion of God we derive from practical reason, in order to 'correct' that notion. But whether this admission is consistent with Kant's general principles seems doubtful.

In general, then, it may be said that Kant's deduction, or recommendation from practical considerations, of the existence of God, though highly suggestive and not, in its positive part, far from the truth, is not a very certain ground for holding the existence of God, and is still less certain when viewed in the context of Kant's whole system.

8

St Thomas's Reasons for Holding the Existence of God

1. *Introductory*

I BEG leave to preface what follows with one or two mile-stones of memory. These will not be of much interest to the Catholic reader but may provide a ray of light for others.

I remember at an early age being shown a well-known picture of St Thomas Aquinas counting off on his fingers his Five Ways of showing the existence of God. I thought at the time that a person would need to be very clever to prove the existence of God, and in five ways; and I did not quite see how anyone would set about it; it did not seem the sort of thing one tried to prove.

At the same age I heard a preacher mention temptations against faith, and this puzzled me because it seemed that a Catholic of normal intelligence with eyes in his head could never have difficulty about the truth of the Church; to do so would be to betray a sort of feeble-mindedness or lack of ordinary powers of observation and appreciation. I have since learnt that this power of appreciation can be lost by Catholics who neglect the grace of God, of which one of the functions is to enlighten the mind about the truths of faith.

At school we were given the Five Ways out of an old-fashioned textbook. There was obviously something unsatisfactory about what I then thought of as the hen-and-the-egg approach, due to what I later came to understand as the different possible levels of insight into contingence. I liked the approach from the order of the world, and have always thought it evident and inescapable; though analysing it reveals a similar difficulty. But this and other difficulties have never for me amounted to a serious doubt about the essential validity of the traditional presentations.

As a student I remember a gifted contemporary once remarking with a laugh that he could not imagine himself ever having any doubts about the faith. One almost never heard a remark like that because normally it seemed something too obvious to say.

At the end of my course of scholastic philosophy I do not think I had a deep grasp of the traditional ways of showing the existence of God, or had seen clearly all the difficulties involved; though I thought the account of the nature of God quite good most of the way. This, while leaving something to learn, seemed good enough to go on with, because it seemed from experience that few if any come to find God by walking in one or other of St Thomas's Five Ways; though since then I have come to see that people could be put off from finding God, or even, if they were not very balanced, shaken in their faith, by philosophical difficulties connected with showing the existence of God. But it seems that oftener than not it is misunderstanding about the nature of God and about our way of knowing Him, rather than difficulty about showing His existence, that causes the trouble. The upshot was that proofs of the existence of God gradually fell into place rather as occupations for those with a philosophical bent, than as something essential to the theist as such. Certainly it would take the average Catholic quite a time to think himself deep into St Thomas's *Pars*

Prima. God help the clever young man who thinks natural theology easy.

The ordinary believer is in a position to say, the world as I know it is very consistent with the existence of God. More than that he scarcely needs, for he is also able to say, the Christian life as I know it is absolutely unthinkable without the existence of God. The philosopher as believer is in the same position as any other believer. As a philosopher he is able to say, the existence of God makes good sense of the world as I see it; to deny the existence of God does not make sense of the world as I see it. But I do not think the reasons he can give are able by themselves to compel anyone's agreement, because at best our insight into finite existence, into the nature of contingence, is limited. If our minds were fully intuitive, it seems that it would be impossible to deny the existence of God. But our minds are not fully intuitive; and therefore at the level of abstract philosophy we can have certainty about the existence of God in the measure in which we can understand finite being as such. This is not without its difficulties, but it can be sufficient because it can exclude prudent doubt. If this is true of the intelligent Catholic whose mental background prepares him to understand the philosophy of God, it will be still more true of the non-Catholic.

I am not, therefore, inclined to usher in the following reasons for holding the existence of God either with a blare of trumpets or with a solemn hush. Some will like them, some will not. There are comparatively few things that can coerce the human mind; almost nothing one might not deny or suspend judgment about, if one felt inclined. Reasons for the existence of God at the level of academic philosophy are no exceptions. They can give sufficient insight to any who will take serious trouble to examine them sympathetically.

But they cannot be coercive because, as I have said, the human mind is not fully intuitive.

Finally, any inquirer who looks on natural theology as simply an academic exercise is not likely to get very far. If God exists, and is what the Catholic claims He is, the objective difference this makes to human life is beyond all calculation and comparison. If there may be someone on the other side of the door, common courtesy requires that we should be ready to meet him.

The process of thought by which St Thomas shows the existence of God is only a deepening and precising of the way the human mind works or can work spontaneously and accurately in considering the world. Few readers of these pages will be quite unacquainted with the two traditional theistic arguments which have come to be known as the Cosmological Argument and the Teleological Argument. The first is an argument from the contingence, that is, the non-necessity, of the world to the existence of a non-contingent or necessary Being who is God. This argument starts with the question whether the world is the sufficient explanation of its own existence; and holds that this is a legitimate question to ask, even if the answer should turn out to be, the world is the sufficient explanation of its own existence, or, it is impossible to say whether the world exists of itself or in dependence on God. The second, the Teleological Argument, in its best form is an argument from the order of the world to the existence of a mind, and ultimately at least, a divine mind, which sets the world in order.

It may come as a surprise in some philosophical circles today, even in some theistic circles, to learn that I propose to defend these two lines of argument as entirely valid. I would only point out that, as I shall presently show by one or two examples, some philosophers who today attack these two lines of thought, especially the first, *ex professo*, have misunderstood them rather badly.

It is a pity that it is hardly practicable to treat the two lines as one, because in fact they are only two aspects of the same thing, and ultimately have exactly the same extension and application. But the reader should try to see all along that they interpenetrate and approach identity. I think myself that the second line of thought, from the order of the world to an intellectual cause, is the easier for the beginner to grasp.

A man looking round the world may well ask himself the question, why does the world exist rather than not exist? If no explanation of the existence of the world is required, then the world is ultimate; and everything, including human beings, has come about by the natural process of evolution, which may be regarded either as something which worked itself out by necessity—it could not happen otherwise—or else by chance, or else by a combination of necessity and chance. This would be extremely wonderful: that chemical elements like hydrogen and carbon, which just happened to be there or just happened to come into being with no cause or reason at all, should, after existing as fiery nebulae, cool, and produce the solar system, the earth, plants and animals in all their variety, and finally man. Extremely wonderful; but to the thoughtful mind not a very satisfying conclusion, but one which must leave a haunting doubt of such proportions that, once faced, it is hard to see how anyone could ever be wholly rid of it.

2. *The Cosmological and Teleological Arguments: formulae and difficulties*

I will now give one or two formulations, some of them good,

others less good, of the two lines of argument I have chosen. For the *Cosmological Argument* there is (i) the well-known formulation of Leibniz as reported by Kant: 'If anything exists, an absolutely necessary being exists. Now, at least I myself exist. Therefore an absolutely necessary being exists.' This formula, though valid, is much too short to be satisfactory. It needs to be shown, besides other things, that an absolutely necessary being is infinite spirit.

(ii) St Thomas in the *Summa Theologica*, 1:2:3, the Third Way. There has been a great deal of discussion about the exact force and sense of the text, but the best way of simplifying the thought would seem to be as follows:

> In the whole of reality there must be something, or some element of reality, that always existed; because if there was ever absolutely nothing, i.e. no world and no God, there would be nothing now. But this permanent thing or element in reality has its permanence either in its own right or else in dependence on some other. But even if we go back through an indefinitely long chain of dependence, we must ultimately postulate a being which has essential and absolute permanence in its own right; and this we call God.

This formula assumes that things cannot come into existence without a cause. It also remains to be shown that a necessary, i.e. essentially permanent, being must be infinite spirit. This St. Thomas does later in his work.

The chief difficulties that can be raised against the Cosmological Argument are (i) those of Kant: that casuality is subjective, and applies only to the material, phenomenal world; that the argument cannot conclude without invoking the false Ontological Argument; that the application of causality leads to an infinite regress and to nothing beyond; that the necessary being which the argument seeks could be the world of our experience. (ii) That the argument cannot get going without assuming its conclusion; for to say that a thing is contingent is *ipso facto* to say that a necessary being exists; because a contingent being means one that depends for its existence on a necessary being. (iii) That 'necessary being' is a nonsense-notion; because necessity belongs only to propositions, not to things; and to hold the existence of a necessary being commits one to holding the Ontological Argument.

The following are some possible formulations of the *Teleological Argument*: (i) St Thomas in the *Summa Theologica*, I :2 :3, the Fifth Way:

> The fifth way is taken from the way things are set in order. We see that certain things which have no intellect, viz. natural bodies, act towards an end, which is evident from the fact that they always, or for the most part, act in the same way, so as to produce what is best. Thus it is clear that they do not act at random, but arrive at the end by being directed to it. But things which have not knowledge do not tend to an end unless directed by one who has knowledge and intellect, as the arrow is directed by the archer. Therefore there is an intelligent cause by which all natural things are ordered towards an end; and this we call God.

This formulation is quite valid but rather vague and needs a good deal of discussion and clarification.

(ii) The analogy from human artefacts: just as we realize without doubt that an alarm-clock needs an intelligent cause, so we realize that, e.g., the body of an animal implies an intelligent cause.

This analogy from human artefacts is complete in all essentials, and entirely valid.

(iii) About anything which has some order or arrangement, it is possible to ask, why is it thus rather than thus?

The immediate answer will be, its nature; and next, the cause or causes that produced the nature. But it is insufficient to go back and back through a never-ending series of causes, unless there is an ultimate cause about which the question, Why is it thus rather than thus? cannot be asked: because, being infinite, it is not thus rather than thus, but is the fullness of being and uncaused.

(iv) There are things in nature which were obviously intended for a purpose, e.g. teeth of different shapes to deal with food in different ways; leaves to protect fruit from excessive heat; eyes to see with, etc. etc. This purpose can have been put into things only by a mind which conceived and caused it.

This formulation, though not invalid in principle, is the least satisfactory in practice.

The chief difficulties that can be brought against this second line of argument are:

(i) Those of Kant: that at best the argument proves that the *order* of the world is dependent, not that the world is dependent 'in its matter or substance', i.e., that it proves only an architect of the universe, not a creator; that to prove the dependence of the matter or substance of the world, recourse must be had to the Cosmological Argument with all its (for Kant) transcendental illusions; that the evidence on which the argument is based is at best only sufficient to prove an ordering mind of great, but not of infinite scope; and finally, that 'finality', or the purpose we imagine natural objects to display, is not objective, though to regard it as objective helps us to unify our apprehension of the world; so that finality is not a 'constitutive' principle of things, but only a 'regulative' principle of our knowledge of things.

(ii) That the argument cannot start without assuming what is to be proved, viz., that the order of the world is due to an intelligent cause. This objection amounts to saying that alternative explanations are possible; that no explanation is needed beyond factors contained in the world, like matter and evolution.

(iii) That at best the argument is too anthropomorphic, and sees the intellect of the transcendent God as working like a finite human intellect. (This objection may sometimes be found, somewhat surprisingly, even in Christian writers; though usually they have in mind a debased form of the argument.)

3. *St Thomas's Five Ways: their nucleus*

As is well known, St Thomas offers five ways of showing the existence of God: the first, from movement to the existence of an unmoved and unchangeable mover; the second, from caused being to an original uncaused cause; the third from 'possible', i.e. non-necessary, being to an absolutely necessary being; the fourth, from degrees of being to being in the highest sense; the fifth, from the way the world is directed to a mind directing the world. Here I want to expound what I take to be the central reason of all the ways, namely, *the insufficiency of finite being as such*. In none of the five ways does St Thomas conclude explicitly to the existence of infinite spirit, but he does so implicitly, leaving the explicit showing of infinity and all that follows from it till later in his work. It will be convenient here to make infinity the explicit conclusion of the argument, which may be summarized as follows:

Finite being is not self-explanatory (*a*) with regard to its own existence (*b*) with regard to its own order;
Finite being requires as its explanation a self-explanatory being; A self-explanatory being is an infinite being.

The argument may now be expanded thus:

4. *Finite existence not self-explanatory*

This is the first point, but in a way it is the whole business. It is certainly the most important point, and perhaps the most difficult. Any finite thing could be non-existent. The sort of thing it is, namely *finite* thing, does not carry with it any necessity for existing. It is possible without contradiction to think of its nature clearly and adequately as either existing or not existing; and this, simply because it is finite being. Thus, I can say with perfect truth that my own nature is such that I need not have existed. I can think of the men of centuries to come, if they do come, as possible men, as not yet existing. I can think of other universes, like this one or unlike it, as not existing. I can think of this universe as having had a beginning. I can, with certain modern scientists, envisage the possibility of hydrogen atoms 'popping into existence', supplying new material for the world; I can think of such a process as starting and as stopping. The conclusion is that finite being as such carries with it no necessity for existence. If it does exist, it is not in virtue of any necessity it has in its own nature as finite being. It is *id cui contingit existere*, that which is lucky enough to exist: what in Thomist language is called contingent being.

A number of points call for further discussion, but I would first point out that here, at the level of philosophy, in so far as one can and should distinguish such levels in human life, we reach what may be called the parting of the ways. The modern mind, when it doubts or denies God's existence or the power of the human mind to find or know

God, will say, it is useless, mere fantasy, to talk of the universe as not requiring existence, as being able not to exist, as only happening to exist, of other universes as being possible, unless you are *assuming* that these things are dependent on a cause which is not part of the universe. The scholastic philosopher replies, No: we have the evidence of our eyes that some things, notably ourselves, come into existence and, so far as their lives here are concerned, pass out of existence. Reflection on this fact enables us to generalize, and to have insight not only at the level of the causes and circumstances of this world which determine whether this or that man will in fact exist, but also at an essentially deeper level, a level which has its application not only to this or that man, but to human nature as such, to material being as such, to finite being as such. To take the one road, to refuse objectivity to any insight of the mind which goes beyond scientific causes, is to exclude the possibility of the existence of God. To take the other road, to admit the objectivity of a deeper insight into the constitution of things than is given by physical science, is to admit the possibility of the existence of God, and implicitly—though not yet explicitly—to affirm it.

The insight claimed as metaphysical, that is, as deeper than physical, which sees the radical insufficiency for existence of finite being as such, is to the human mind a spontaneous pressure but, taken by itself, difficult to assess and comparatively easy to starve. When combined with the intelligibility, order, beauty of the world, it becomes a stronger pressure. It would seem that the mind spontaneously, inevitably, tends to see the intelligibility of the world as directly reflecting an intellect which sets order, and this order rather than that, into the universe.

I do not know whether anything else can be done than

to set these two states of mind face to face and let them speak for themselves. I have called it a parting of the ways. It involves a decision not quickly or lightly to be made. Men are involved in a similar parting of the ways when, looking into history, they meet Christ's claim; and when, looking around them, they meet Christ's Church.

5. *The meaning of 'contingent'*

On a point of terminology, some Thomists would take one to task for including finite spirit under contingent things; because finite spirit, unlike material things, cannot cease to be what it is as an apple can cease to be an apple. Finite spirit, once it exists, cannot cease to exist as finite spirit— unless it is annihilated by God; and therefore St Thomas calls a finite spirit a 'necessary' thing, and a material thing, by contrast, a 'possible' thing. But this is a matter of terminology, and I find it convenient to follow a not un-common practice and use the word contingent of anything that is not of its nature absolutely bound to exist.

It is sometimes objected, even by some Catholic philo-sophers, that to say that a thing is contingent is to say that God exists, because a contingent thing *means* a thing that depends on God for its existence. But this objection plays on the different levels of meaning of the word 'contingent'. 'Capable of existing or not existing' is certainly not the same *meaning* as 'depending on God for existence', however true it may be that the former ultimately implies the latter. Contingence has several different layers of meaning. Let us try to sort them out. Contingent could mean: (*a*) 'able to exist or not exist' as these words are used of, say, next year's apple-crop or of an apple which someone eats. These processes St Thomas would call substantial change, and this, with the lesser types of change called accidental change, as when an apple changes colour, are the only *observable* elements of contingence.

(*b*) But, however true it is that the apple ceases to exist, this type of contingence is not the same as if the apple were to become nothing—to be totally annihilated. Contingence in that sense is never observed. If we hold it for a possibility, it is because we conclude to it with the mind, not see it with the eyes. If a scientist holds that there is no contradiction in hydrogen atoms 'popping into existence', he is saying that there is no contradiction in the idea of contingence in this second sense. If there is nothing contradictory in the passage from nothing to something, presumably there is none in the passage from something to nothing. Of course, the scientist as such has his own canons and methods, and they are not identical with those of natural theology. I am here only illustrating the second layer of the meaning of contingence. If a person holds that there is nothing contradictory in the idea of the universe passing into sheer nothingness, he is envisaging its contingence in this second sense; and it is a sense that is different from that of the contingence of an apple which someone eats.

(*c*) Contingence could imply, further, that a thing which could be nothing must have a cause in order to be something—a cause of its starting to exist, if it did start to exist, and also, a still further point, a cause on which it depends for existence here and now. This, of course, would be questioned by some, so that it would appear that 'able to exist or not exist' has not got exactly the same meaning as 'depending on a cause for beginning to exist and for existing here and now'.

(*d*) If a person grants that a thing can come into existence out of nothing only under the influence of a cause, he might argue that this universe was caused by a previous universe which has now ceased to exist; or he might say that the first universe was not caused but just given; or he might say it was in turn caused by a previous universe, and so on *ad infinitum*; or he might try to invoke circular causality.

But if a person is such a quick philosopher that he sees: that this universe, because it is finite, can be thought of as non-existent; that this implies that its actual existence is not self-explanatory; that this implies that it had and has a cause; that any number of finite causes, even an infinite number of them, is not a sufficient explanation, and in fact gets us not one step nearer to an explanation; that the only sufficient explanation of the universe is a cause which is also self-explanatory, and that a self-explanatory cause cannot cease to exist and must be infinite spirit—if he can see all this at a glance, so much the better. He can see, by a consideration of the universe, that there exists a being identical with what Christians understand by God. But it seems a little over-hasty to suggest that because a person can hold that there is nothing contradictory in this apple being eaten, in this grain of sand not existing, or even in the whole universe not existing—to suggest that to know the meaning of contingent in that sense is *the same thing as* to know that there exists a self-explanatory being, infinite spirit, on whom the universe here and now depends.

This contingence in existence is not to be confused with contingence in action. A free act, the choosing of X, is contingent in so far as the agent could have chosen not-X; but besides that, there is the contingence of the agent, which means that there need not have been any agent to choose either X or not-X.

The world is, as a matter of fact, contingent in the sense that creation is a free choice of God. The existence of God follows from the existence of the world; but the existence of the world does not follow from the existence of God.

No good is done by ignoring the initial difficulty that the mind feels in accepting the contingence of the whole universe, or by ignoring the difference between the contingence of the whole universe and the contingence of an apple that somebody eats; and some forms of the 'argument from contingence' do tend to gloss over this difference. However true it is that every item of the universe can cease to be the sort of thing it is, and even if every item in the universe is supposed to be contingent in that sense, still, the universe as a whole obstinately clings to existence. From one point of view the universe is a collection of material things, very changeable but very indestructible. Thus the scientist may see it, and even for the philosopher, in material things the corruption of one thing is *ipso facto* the generation of another. Such is the initial difficulty, and only long pondering can dispel it. We are so accustomed to coming-to-be and passing-away in the ordinary sense that it does not seem surprising. But in itself it is highly surprising and mysterious, so much so that Parmenides, a great mind and no mere paradox-monger, concluded that it could not happen. We take change for granted, but in itself it is as mysterious and surprising as creation or annihilation; the latter seems more difficult only because we never see it. For St Thomas, as for Aristotle, all the actuality a thing has comes from the form, the factor that determines the matter. Pure matter is pure potentiality, nothing actual, not a thing but a component of material things. It is the peculiarity of material things that the disappearance of one form necessarily involves the appearance of another. But no particular form is necessarily present in the matter. Every particular form is contingent, thus making the *thing*, the combination of matter and form, a contingent thing. The more the contingence of the individual material thing is really understood in the light of the theory of matter and form, the less the difference appears between the emergence of a new substance and creation. New intelligibility, and therefore new being, arises at every moment. If this involves new substance, the only permanence is the substratum, pure matter, which is no actuality but only potentiality for the reception of forms.

However, difficulty is felt by some scholastic philosophers in allowing that there are distinct material things at all. It can be argued that the whole material universe is one material substance, and that any change that takes place within it is accidental, not substantial. If this is so, the contingence of this one substance cannot be known from its beginning to be, but must be shown in some other way. If beginning to be is taken as a sign of contingence, it is best to take the example of man who, by virtue of his spiritual form, is undoubtedly a distinct individual substance. Each man need not have existed; there is a man where there could have been no man.

The contingence of the universe can be approached indirectly as follows. In asking whether the universe is self-explanatory, we can begin by asking what sort of a thing would be one whose existence was self-explanatory, which contained in itself the answer to the question, Why does it exist? In answer it can be shown that such a being would be one whose existence is not adventitious, not a happy accident, but whose nature is so inseparable from existence as to be identical with it. It can be shown that such a being is infinite spirit and absolutely unchangeable. But the universe is neither infinite in being, nor pure spirit, nor unchangeable; therefore the existence of the universe is not self-explanatory. At this point it is not unusual for the wary

reader to cry, 'Ha! the Ontological Argument! You have
assumed that infinite spirit is possible. But, as you have
admitted and shown, if infinite spirit is possible, then it
exists; that is, you have assumed the existence of God.' The
objection is unfounded. It has not been claimed at this stage
that a self-explanatory being is either required or possible.
It has only been said that if there were such a thing as a
self-explanatory being, it would be such and such. The
possibility is still open that a self-explanatory being is neither
necessary nor possible; the necessity and possibility of the
conception are established only indirectly, only when comparison has actually been made with finite being and it has
been seen that here is a reality that needs explanation and
cannot explain itself. Even if the notion of self-explanatory being, of infinite spirit, is a contradiction in terms,
it would still have terms; and the terms would be sufficient to allow the conclusion that this universe is not
self-explanatory; just as we can say that the sun is not of
infinite size, even though we may doubt whether it is possible for anything to be of infinite size. On the other hand, it
must not be assumed at the outset that self-explanatory
being, infinite spirit, is *im*possible. If the concept is well-
behaved at first, that, so far, is a recommendation. But, as
has been pointed out in dealing with the Ontological
Argument, we cannot tell, merely by inspection of the
concept of God, whether God is possible or not. The existence of a material universe is, then, on this showing, not
self-explanatory, because if it were so, the universe would be
infinite spirit and unchangeable. But once more, if the
reader, accepting the principles and their application, sees
at once that a self-explanatory being is required, so much
the better; he sees at once that God exists.

This indirect approach to the contingence of finite things

is not really different from the one first given. A finite thing, because it is finite, can be thought of adequately as a nature that is a blank essence without existence. The sort of thing it is does not demand existence; if it does exist, this is not in virtue of anything its nature demands. On the other hand, if a thing is existent of its very nature, it cannot be finite and must be infinite. In a finite being alone is there room for the distinction, even in thought, between essence and existence. It might be objected that infinite being can be thought of as existent or non-existent as easily as finite being can. This is quite true; and the reason is that infinite being cannot be thought of by a finite mind directly at all; but we can judge that such must be its nature, and that if we could know it directly we should know it as being without restriction or qualification: infinite existence.

Such is an attempt to explain the Thomist notion of contingence at one level of its meaning—the level at which it can be said that a finite thing, even a universe of finite things, does not have existence of its own nature. It would be a mistake to claim that the notion is an easy one to grasp at first, even, it would seem, for those who have given the philosophy of St Thomas some considerable sympathetic study. The scientist as such quite rightly takes the world as he finds it; he is concerned with observable, measurable facts and their interconnections within the universe. Certain philosophers go further and claim that philosophy should approach or even be identified with physical science; and that what cannot be explained by the methods, canons and categories of physical science cannot be explained at all. For them, the question whether the universe is self-explanatory does not arise; the universe is simply given, and nothing more can be said on the point: what is beyond our experience has, they claim, no meaning. One could, of course, agree while pointing out that the possibility is still open that these philosophers will come face to face with God in a few years' time. This they are not disposed to allow; so that to ask them to understand the Thomist conception of contingence as so far defined, is to ask for the moon.

6. *The Teleological Argument*

Finite order not self-explanatory. So far I have been defending the view that the existence of a finite universe is not self-explanatory. I now turn to the parallel consideration, that the *order* of the universe is not self-explanatory. Of course, if the existence of the universe is not self-explanatory, neither is its order; but one can with profit take the two points separately, as I hope to show.

Historically, to most people and to many philosophers, the order of the universe has appeared to be a strong reason for postulating a mind directing it—a mind either in the universe or distinct from it. Nowadays, apart from scholastic philosophers, who have always upheld the validity of this argument, most philosophers would doubt or deny it, largely under the influence of Kant. It is now commonly taken for granted that Kant's explanation of finality must be the classical starting-point for any further treatment of the subject.

Such scientists as are not interested in theism commonly hold that the order of the universe is sufficiently accounted for by evolution and natural selection. Some, however, feel that a difficulty remains; that apart from man, mind must be found somewhere in the universe; and it has been proposed that all matter has a mental factor, and that perhaps molecules can think and direct themselves.

Among the ancient Greeks, the atomists in the strict

sense, those who held ultimate particles unchangeable in quality and shape, held that the universe was formed by the chance collocation of different kinds of particles. The modern evolutionary theory is different in so far as it is understood today that matter has a number of definite and distinct powers; that the universe is a vast and complicated system of laws of behaviour; that there are definite kinds of atoms which can combine into definite kinds of molecules so as to produce even living things. These powers the scientist calls 'laws of nature' and as a scientist quite rightly leaves it at that.

Even if it is admitted that a mind is at work in the universe, it still has to be shown that this mind is not merely some part of the universe, a 'soul of the world' such as the Stoics held, or some quasi-souls in material things, or some rudimentary consciousness in things which would enable them to combine and form the universe we know. As I have said, all scholastic philosophers hold that the argument is entirely valid at least to the extent of showing the existence of a mind distinct from the universe and the cause of its order. Even if it should be necessary to show the existence of *infinite* mind by some other way, still, to show directly that there is a mind at all is a great point gained. As St Thomas concludes: 'Therefore there is something with intellect by which all natural things are directed to an end; and this we call God.'

Finality: the problem. In the whole history of philosophy few notions have been beset with as much confusing undergrowth as the notion of finality; and some surprisingly obstinate controversy among scholastic philosophers concerning the principle of finality suggests that they are not entirely exempt from the confusion. The very words 'finality', 'teleology' have remote and teasing overtones;

while the word 'purpose' has something question-begging about its very sound. If we say that the principle of finality states that 'every agent acts for an end', or 'because of an end', or 'with an end in view', or 'for a purpose', we do not feel very enlightened or reassured. Do we say that a stone falls in order to reach the ground? If so, what on earth do we mean? Do we say that an acorn grows in order to become an oak-tree? How do we know? And what is an end? The end of an oak-tree is its death and dissolution; so does it grow in order to die?

If we read in Cicero[1] that the muscular necks and shoulders of oxen were evidently designed by nature to carry the yoke and pull the plough, we may feel we have reached the border between sense and nonsense. Shall we say that a pleasant stretch of river is intended by nature, or by anything else, as a good place for a picnic—or not? And if it comes to order, the pebbles on the shore are all round and smooth: is this design, intention, or is it the natural result of the action of the waves? If we look at the stars and see Orion the hunter or Cassiopeia's throne or the Plough, we are evidently reading into them an order that is not objective; they just happen to look like that from the earth, and we choose to group them in that way; it is no more objective design than if a cloud happens to look like a camel. Then, to take an example from a classical champion of teleology, is it obvious that leaves are meant to protect fruit? Aristotle was one of the foremost upholders of teleology, and for very good reasons; but his mighty river of thought seems to end in a marsh when we find that the purpose in the world is unconscious striving towards a goal, a metaphorical, 'mythical' purpose with, apparently, no mind directed towards it and so directing it. And is it not

[1] *De Natura Deorum*, II, 159.

true that the Iliad could be formed by chance by Greek letters falling one by one out of a sack? As a matter of fact it is true, and the mathematician could give you the amount of time necessary for the possibility to become a practical certainty. Then, is it true or is it not, that half a dozen monkeys with typewriters could eventually type out every book in the British Museum?

Evidently we shall have to pick our way carefully in this matter.

The Principle of Finality is usually worded, *omne agens agit propter finem*, 'every agent acts for an end'. If we know that God exists, that He has given things their natures, and that through these natures He directs things in their activities so that they will produce individually, and combine to produce corporately, the effects He intends to be produced in the world, the principle of finality is, of course, evidently true. But the question is, is it evident *before* God's existence is known that things act 'for an end' in the sense of 'for an end that is foreseen and intended by a mind'? I answer that it is so evident, or, more accurately, that the existence of a directing mind is immediately implied by a consideration of the action of things; but that in showing this, it is no help but rather a hindrance to start from the thing's action: much better to concentrate on the thing's being, on what it *is* rather than on what it *does*.

In considering finality one can start by examining actions or by examining results, but in either case both must be included. A finite thing is the result of action; the thing in turn proceeds to other actions and results. St Thomas, in treating of finality, seems mostly to concentrate on action rather than being; but it is easy to see that he intends to include both action and being, as he must. I am inclined to think that the discord among scholastic philosophers in interpreting St Thomas on this point is produced by for-getting in practice what would be admitted in theory—that the finality revealed in finite action is not really separable from the finality revealed in finite being; they are both parts of the phenomenon called finite order. Moreover, action is a more difficult concept than being, and its in-herent difficulties seem to lead to unnecessary confusion when action is used as a focal point to illustrate finality. I should prefer to reword the principle of finality as follows: *omne ens finitum est finis alicuius intentionis*—all finite being, whether thing or action, is the result of intelligent intention or direction.

The showing of the existence of mind on which the universe depends amounts simply to this, that the order of the universe, both in what it is and in what it does, could have been absent; instead of order there could have been comparative disorder; instead of this order there could have been different order; and the cause which makes the dif-ference between order and disorder, between this order and some other, cannot be less than a mind of very great intelli-gence; and this mind is not part of the universe itself.

The actual order of the universe scarcely needs stressing for any reflective mind, though we tend to take it for granted. By order I mean *intelligibility* at the levels at which intelligibility is available—the levels of common observa-tion and of the sciences concerned with living and non-living things and with men. The greater the intelligibility, the greater the perfection of being; and the intelligibility of the observable universe has not yet been exhausted by any human mind individually, or corporately by all the greatest minds the world has so far seen.

The universe as we know it includes order and also what we call disorder. The order is that of inorganic matter and its combinations, from those investigated by astronomy down to the structure of the atom; the order of plants and animals in their families, genera and species; and the perfection which in a manner includes all else and more besides —the human intellect. What is called disorder is mostly if not exclusively the result of combinations of these ordered things which for one reason or another we do not like: the harm done directly or indirectly by the elements, through rain, sun, storms and earthquakes; by poisonous plants and noxious animals; by disease and death; by men among themselves; and disorder within the individual man. From the first point of view it is said to be order, and good; from the second, we tend to say it is disorder, and bad. The second point of view I have tried to deal with in treating of the problem of evil; I am concerned here with the first.

Not all combinations of things are disorderly. Inorganic matter, terrestrial and cosmic, is interconnected in a system whose unity becomes more and more apparent to the scientist; and the greater the unity-in-diversity the greater the perfection. Plants could not live without inorganic matter, moisture, heat and light; animals could not live without plants; men could not live without air, plants and animals; men could not live without material things to meet their senses. In spite of many apparent disorders and enormous hazards, plants, animals and men have survived on the earth, and the whole has developed into a universe that evidently includes order, goodness, unity, beauty, great in proportion to its intelligibility. It is with this intelligibility that I am now concerned.

Perfection-in-combination is very evident; but there is also imperfection-in-combination; so it will be better to consider 'internal' finality, as it is called, rather than 'external' finality. External finality is the goodness-in-combination of things; internal finality is the perfection or order of individual things considered as made up of a complexus of parts and functions. Nothing, therefore, will be said about the usefulness of things—about wool for clothing, plants for food, rain for crops, though the scientist realizes that a great deal could be said. It will be amply sufficient to consider the order of the universe as it exists in separate things—in inorganic matter, in the vegetable and animal kingdoms, and in man.

But there is an initial difficulty about this approach. It may be objected that it is unreal to pick and choose in this way. In the treatment of the problem of evil it was suggested that, though the situation may be bad for the individual here and now, the function of the individual transcends its individual self, transcends the here and now; that we cannot know what an individual thing *is* except in relation to a much wider whole, cannot know it perfectly except in its relation to the end result of the whole universe. In the same way it may be said that individual things or groups of things, the subject-matter of chemistry, astronomy, botany, zoology, may show wonderful order and seem very good in isolation, but their good order and their functions can only be assessed in the light of the whole universe, and not merely here and now, but in its final result; and the final result is beyond our experience and calculation; and in so far as it *is* available to our calculation, it is evident that the order is offset by a good deal of what seems to be disorder, of combinations that are not evidently good, of the spoiling of individual perfection and attractiveness in a welter of unintelligibility; and if *one* mind is held responsible for the order, it must also be responsible for the apparent and admittedly impenetrable disorder.

This is a good objection, but I would make here only one

point: there are only two possible alternatives, that the universe is directed by mind and that it is not; and I am concerned to show that the first alternative is the right one. What is concluded about the nature of this mind is a further point, though an important one.

It is a curious fact that natural things and groups of things taken in isolation present examples of remarkable and wellnigh perfect order. The various natural sciences, astronomy, chemistry, physics, botany, zoology, are sheer delight to the mind for the perfection of their subject-matter. It is when different orders of things are seen in combination that the difficulty starts. We are hardly puzzled by the fact that plants live and die and that plants are eaten by animals and men; we may not be very puzzled by what at first looks like waste in the vegetable and animal kingdoms; but we are puzzled by disease, by blighting of the crops by which men and animals live, by disease in animals, by their natural preying upon one another, by what seems like unnecessary suffering in animals, and most of all by the miseries of men in their dependence on lower nature. It looks as though the higher one goes in nature, the more the individual and species, in proportion to their inherent perfection, are subject to hazards and imperfections.

Most wonderful of all in his own nature is man, because by his intellect he is able to become, to make his own mentally, everything in the universe, and to invent more things for himself. And he is able not only to know these things but also to judge them. If there is a mind that orders the universe and made man, this mind has put itself very much at the mercy of the minds it has made, giving man enormous power and corresponding responsibility. One may reflect on the greatness and the limitations of the human mind. Men can make things which it is not absurd to compare for beauty and goodness with the works of nature. But in doing so, man is really extolling the wonders of nature, including himself. Nature is his inspiration directly or indirectly. Even in music he expresses his own mind and feelings as enriched by nature. The architecture of music is in some strange way a reflection of the architecture which informs and satisfies us as men; and this in turn is analogous to the architecture of the universe by which all is sustained in a unity. Man expresses these things in music because he finds them beautiful, sometimes in themselves, sometimes because he has transformed them and made new beauty on their model through the alchemy of his insight. But this mind of man is part of nature; man did not plan it and make it. He can develop it, but he does so by enriching it from the stores of nature and from his own and other people's experience of nature and of themselves.

A great mind is a gift, however much its development is due to its possessor. We can no more command our mental gifts than our physical. Mind, then, is by far the most wonderful part of nature; and man did not make it. It seems also to be the only part of nature that can easily harm itself as well as other things. This suggests caution and a certain humility. We can spoil our own minds, condition them for better or for worse, not merely as instruments for knowing but as parts of ourselves, as instruments for judging, interpreting meaning, assessing good and evil. If we realize that there is more intelligibility in the world than we are capable of knowing, it is not unreasonable to think that there is more intelligibility than we are capable of judging. Very strangely, the higher we go in the scale of being, the more acute the problem of evil becomes, till it reaches its climax in man. Is this essentially a lowering of intelligibility? Or is it a heightening of intelligibility which our minds find it hard to keep pace with? If we hardly know what is matter, are we better placed to be confident about the question, what is man?

But when all is said, one thing remains: it is certain that the ordering of the universe is the work of intellect apart from the universe; and that without intellect, all the alternatives that have been proposed—chance, evolution, necessity, immanent form, rudimentary consciousness—are insufficient.

First, the order of the universe is not absolutely necessary. If it were so, it could not possibly be absent or different. We know that it could be absent and different at least to this extent, that it was not always present. It has evolved, in our part of the universe, from simplicity to great complexity, from comparative poverty to great richness, from mere materiality to the appearance of life and mind. Again, obviously, we can change the order of the world to a large extent, controlling and modifying species of animals and plants and working minerals and, quite possibly, blowing up continents. It is true that so long as matter remains, some order remains, because matter as we know it, even when reduced to atoms and less, has a high degree of internal order. It was thought not long ago that the atom was physically ultimate and unchangeable; we now know to our cost that it is not.

The point I am making is exactly parallel to the one I made under the heading *Finite being not self-explanatory*, and leads to a similar parting of the ways. Finite order, finite intelligibility, is not self-explanatory. Reflection on the order we know and on the way we see it change, leads immediately to the conclusion that finite order *as such* could be different and could be absent; and the fact that it is present, and is this order rather than that, points immediately to the conclusion that it is selected and imposed by some mind somewhere. The only alternative is an impossible one: that matter is as great as mind, because it is its cause.

Once again the two views may be set face to face and allowed to speak for themselves. On the one side are those who say: You cannot claim that the order of the universe or any finite order could be absent or could be different unless you are *assuming* that there is an intelligent cause, and ultimately an infinite intelligent cause, capable of producing the difference between order and its absence, between this order and some other. But, the upholders of this view go on, we can get along very well without this assumption, by holding that the *de facto* order of the universe and its development are simply given and ultimate, and there is neither need nor possibility of asking any further question about its origin. Order and intelligibility *can* be different only if there is a cause capable of producing the difference. If there is no such cause, your claim that they can be different is mere imagination, mere space-fiction. On the other hand, the scholastic philosopher replies: It is not a matter of 'This order could be absent or could be other than it is *if* there were a cause capable of making it so', but 'Because I see that finite order, of its very idea and radical nature is not necessarily present and need not be the kind of order that it is, I know concomitantly that it has a cause which made it to be order rather than disorder, this order rather than some other.'

It should be noticed that to say the order of the universe is not absolutely necessary is not to deny that it is determined in its behaviour. Granted the elements out of which the universe is evolving, and granted the emergence of life, which seems to set a special problem, then, apart from the free will of man, there is no reason to deny that the universe had to evolve in exactly the way it does. But this necessity of behaviour of material things, which is called determinism, is quite different from an alleged necessity of existence of these natures rather than some others, of more or less of them, which would have evolved in some other way.

The order of the universe not explained by chance.

It would be a thankless task to try to meet the various advocates of the chance-hypothesis because, though it is a philosophical question and not a scientific, those who today advance the hypothesis do not usually do so in the context of philosophical principles, but only in the context of scientific hypothesis which, as everyone knows, is always revisable. The chance-hypothesis could mean: the existence and behaviour of the universe is ultimate, and it is no use asking questions about it. It might have come out of nothing without any cause, or it might have been always there. The stuff it is made of might have developed in any way at all; it just does not concern us. We can know nothing of what is possible or impossible except by scientific investigation which tells us simply what did, in fact, happen. Or again, the view that the order of the universe 'happened by chance' might be envisaged in the context of the definite behaviour of elementary matter as known to science, on the following lines: There always existed, or there began to exist, atoms of some kind, or some still simpler elements. These had their own laws of behaviour, and whereas these laws result for the most part in very little development, it so happens that in the solar system, on the earth, the conditions were just right for their development into a greatly enhanced perfection, so as to produce life—plants and animals in all their variety, and finally men. No mind started or guided the process: the inherent laws and powers of matter are all that need be invoked. It is as though one said, there is no reason why a cloud should look like a camel, and no reason why it should not; and if it does, it need cause no surprise. And so, there is no reason why atoms of the various elements should combine to produce a camel, and no reason why they should not, because in fact they do; and if they do, there is nothing to be surprised about.

The chance-hypothesis is refuted fundamentally by the consideration that pure chance is literally inconceivable. For, chance is the conjunction of factors, elements, causes, to produce a result which, so far as we can judge, is not intentional. But the factors or elements themselves are already highly ordered things; they have their own natures and regular behaviour, and this, even in the simplest elements, involves a high degree of order and intelligibility. So that the original question remains, no matter how far we push it back. Without order of some kind, nothing could exist or be conceived; it could not have enough stability or permanence to be either thinkable or existent. It is impossible, therefore, to speak of chance without at the same time speaking of order, no matter how much we simplify the elements that are said to combine by chance.

This looks like saying that order cannot be absent from the universe, which would seem to contradict its contingence. That is true only in the sense that ultimately order and existence are in the concrete inseparable to the point of identity. The extinction of order is the extinction of existence.

Order is existence seen as intelligibility; and if it is objective order and not merely an order that my mind reads arbitrarily into things, I hope to show that as such, whether simple or complex, it is necessarily the work of mind. As contingent existence it requires a cause; as contingent intelligible existence it requires an intelligent cause. But this is to anticipate. So far it is claimed that pure chance is

inconceivable, and therefore cannot be the whole explanation of the order of the world.

Let us now see whether chance in a relative sense can
account for the development of order: whether, granted
atoms or something even simpler, the world we know of
inorganic matter, of plants, animals and men, could be due
to the chance collocation of such elements.

The complex order of living things arose, in fact, because certain elements could and did form new and much
more complex combinations. Chemically speaking, all
living things, even the human body, are made up of the
same elements as inorganic matter, but the molecule of
living things is far more complex than that of non-living.
On the face of it this could mean either that inorganic
matter has intrinsically the power, given certain conditions,
of forming new combinations; or that life requires a special
intervention, a cause that is not part of the material world,
to form the first new living things or combinations necessary
for their development, just as metal can combine to form an
alarm-clock, but not without external intervention. The
scientist as such may not unreasonably assume that the first
alternative is possible, and that given the requisite conditions living cells and living things could be formed in the
laboratory; though with all the resources of modern chemistry he has not yet succeeded in doing this. If all material
things are absolutely determined in their behaviour, determined by antecedent causes and by their own natures to act
and develop in this way and in no other, then the whole
process of evolution was determined from the first; physically speaking it could not happen otherwise—until the
advent of man who has free will and is not absolutely determined in his behaviour by his antecedents, his nature, or his
surroundings. If the view that physical things are thus

determined is correct, the view that the order of things is due to chance is ruled out in the sense that chance is now identical with physical necessity, but not with absolute necessity. I think that the view that matter is completely determined is the right one on philosophical grounds, though the scientist as such accepts it only as a more or less probable hypothesis; he does not prove it, because its proof would be a matter of philosophy, not of science.

The ancient Greek with little science, and the American Indian with none, had all the equipment necessary to conclude that the order of the universe is not to be attributed to chance and is to be attributed to mind. This conclusion can be arrived at by thinking carefully without any further reference to physical science than is needed for looking at the world. The principles involved are, that the order of the world is not absolutely necessary; that there could have been relatively extreme disorder; and that chance even in a relative sense cannot explain the order. The last principle is usually applied by analogy with human artefacts, and the analogy is entirely valid. No one imagines for a moment that the paintings of buffaloes in the caves of Altamira are there by chance. If one spoke to the investigator of 'one chance in untold millions', and warned him that he was being utterly unscientific in drawing conclusions about early man, he would have no patience with one. But if the paintings are not there by chance, much less are the buffaloes themselves. To assume that the paintings *must* be the work of minds and that the buffaloes *need not* be the work of mind is to exclude the explanation of mind not for want of evidence but simply *a priori*.

This line of thought need have nothing to do with the usefulness of things, their 'purpose' in that sense—unless, indeed, one were to extend the meaning of 'useful' to include

everything intelligible, and say that everything, by being
intelligible, is useful to our minds. It is the mere intelligibility of natural things that indicates mind as their cause;
what only mind can grasp requires mind as its adequate
explanation. And the order is objective; we do not merely
read it into things; we find it laboriously and submit to it.
Intelligibility is the same as perfection of being. In material
things it is the unity of parts and functions into one whole,
the goodness of the thing's self, apart from its usefulness to
anything else. To see a great, complex machine working
with perfect precision is to see something intelligible, good,
satisfying to the mind, even though we know nothing of
what the machine is for. That is what the cave-painters
found in nature: things good, intelligible, able to hold the
mind in contemplation. By painting they paid tribute to
nature, including their own minds as the highest product of
nature. Mind is the supreme example of order in nature
because it is ordered to the understanding of all that is and
can be.

To invoke chance, even in a relative sense, to explain the
order of the world, is to invoke what would be rejected in
every other department of life and investigation. When four
bridge-players each get a complete suit of cards, they write
to papers about it. If a bridge-player invariably dealt himself a complete suit of trump cards he would not be called a
lucky man. But the whole universe, and most obviously the
whole world of living things, is orderly in that way, but with
incomparably greater perfection and with incomparably
more separate factors involved. Much more: when many
elements come together in ordered unity, not momentarily,
or as a static agglomeration, but stay together and work
together as a unity, it is no longer possible to invoke 'one
chance in untold millions' any more than it is possible to

explain an alarm-clock that way. The permanent working together of many elements, themselves indifferent to that collation, means that they have been made to overcome not merely very many chances of disorder but unlimited chances of disorder. This can be seen from one point of view by considering the unlimited divisibility of time and movement; even in a short time there is unlimited possibility of any dynamic, unified order lapsing into disorder. That it does not do so when absolutely speaking it could indicates that the possibility of the order's being due to chance is not merely very remote but less than any assignable quantity. To pursue such a 'possibility' is to attempt to overtake one's shadow.

The order of the universe caused by mind

If the order of the universe cannot be explained adequately either by necessity or by chance, it can only be explained by the choice of a free agent; and a free agent can only be an intellectual agent. This applies to every objective order, even inorganic; and all the more to living things, and most of all to men. The adequate cause of intellect cannot be less than intellect; the lesser perfection cannot be the adequate cause of the greater; what is not cannot explain what is.

Thus *instinct* as found in any animals or in all animals together cannot explain its own order or the order of the world. Instinct is not intellect, for if it were it would see not only the type of actions to which it is determined, but every possible type of action; it would be indefinitely adaptable, as man is, not merely adaptable within strict limits like the bee. So instinct cannot understand itself and cannot produce itself. It is a type of activity that is chosen for it and imposed on it by a mind; just as a machine has a type of activity chosen for it and imposed on it by its human maker.

Much less is some rudimentary consciousness in the elements of matter sufficient to explain the order of the universe. The only possible reason for postulating such consciousness when all the appearances are against it would be in order to explain the order of the world. Some scientists have postulated it for that reason, thus admitting that neither the necessity of matter nor chance are sufficient.

In the history of philosophy there have been a number of attempts to place the intellect that directs the world within the world itself and nowhere else. The Greeks, as I have mentioned, tended to think of the world as one big living thing. Even Plato, who held the existence of God apart from the world, describes God as giving the world a soul. This is understandable up to a point. It is a tribute to the interrelated unity which early philosophers saw in the universe—a unity which in many respects has been amply confirmed by modern science. To make the world one big *living* thing sounds strange to us, because however much unity it has, it does not look to us like one thing, or one living thing. However much unity it has, and however much the analogy is pressed between cosmic evolution and the development of an individual living organism, we continue to hold that the material universe has neither the kind of unity nor the behaviour we attribute to one living thing. Not the unity: for men, at least, though in their bodies they are part of the material universe, in their immaterial souls are independent of it and able to assert their independence by using their free wills and changing it. The universe has not the behaviour of one living thing. The picture of the universe as a whole as presented, e.g., by the contemporary theory of an expanding universe, is no more like the behaviour we attribute to a living thing than is the explosion of an atom bomb. It is orderly movement and differentiation, but not one life.

Even if the universe could be regarded as one living thing on the animal level, it could not be regarded as possessing intellect. It does not behave in the least like a thing with conscious intellect, an essential characteristic of which is freedom of choice. But the material universe is found to be everywhere determined in its behaviour, at least with statistical determinism; and it is impossible to regard sub-atomic particles as intelligent units. At the other extreme is the view of Absolute Idealism, which found in the universe not matter at all, but one great ultimate Spirit or Idea, evolving inexorably towards greater and greater perfection. But absolute intellect cannot evolve, cannot change, cannot develop; and cannot include evil. If intellect can change and develop, it is finite, not absolute; and, as finite, itself requires an infinite cause as its ultimate explanation. However, at this stage the important point is the conclusion that intellect, and nothing less, is the ultimate cause of the order of the universe.

It is sometimes objected that evolution can explain the order of the world in such a way as to exclude the necessity of intellect. In fact, however, evolution makes not the slightest difference to the case one way or the other, except, perhaps, to emphasize the fact that the order of the world is not absolutely necessary, that it is possible for it to be absent, and that there was a time when relatively speaking it was absent. The enumeration of the physical causes and processes which have produced the order of the world is the enumeration of the facts that need explanation, of what cannot be explained without a directing intellect; just as the description of the processes of cooking without reference to cooks cannot explain the Lord Mayor's dinner. Some would complain that we see cooks but do not see God. This only amounts to saying that what we cannot see does not exist; a shallow conclusion. We cannot see what goes on in the cook's mind, but we still think it important. 'Natural selection' means that certain changes which arose in living things were 'selected for survival'; that is, the conditions in nature were such that these changes did, in fact, survive and were perpetuated by reproduction. Other changes survived for a longer or a shorter time and have now ceased to exist. It has often been pointed out quite rightly that natural selection can only select; and that the mutations from which selection is made by 'nature' are precisely the orderly things that need explanation. The same is often true of the mutations which did not survive. They could have produced, and they often did produce for a time, types which were just as orderly as those which survived longer and still survive. Those which did not survive were not always mere disorder; and even when they were, to reject them and select the rest is a work of order and of mind, just as when a cook rejects a bad plum. Moreover, the 'nature' which does the selecting, that is, the *de facto* physical conditions of evolution, is simply one aspect of the order of the universe which needs explaining. To give names to the order in its various aspects—'nature', 'instinct', 'mutations', 'natural selection', 'laws of nature', 'evolution'—is to name what is to be explained, not to explain it any more than the menu explains the Lord Mayor's dinner.

For my own part I confess that I cannot understand how anyone who has ever looked attentively at one sparrow's feather could imagine for a moment that the universe is ordered by chance in any meaning of that fluid term.

7. *Conclusion*

So far I have defended the positions that finite being is not self-explanatory with regard to its own existence; and that the order of the universe is not self-explanatory, but can only be explained by a mind that is not part of the universe. That this mind, if not itself infinite, in turn depends ultimately on an infinite mind, follows from the first position defended, if it be granted that infinite being is infinite mind, as shown in Part Two of this essay.

The conclusion to infinite being in general may be elaborated a little more as follows.

If no finite being explains its own existence, no series of finite beings, not even an infinite series, explains the existence of any finite thing, or of the whole series. An infinite series of finite causes would still be in the region of finite being, just as an infinite number of bricks would still have the nature of brick and nothing more.

Whether an infinite series of finite causes is possible or not—existing simultaneously or not, in actual causal subordination or not—makes no difference at all to the argument.

There is no contradiction in calling God the First Cause, yet allowing that an infinite series of finite causes is possible, even though an infinite series of finite causes would have no first finite cause. God would not be part of such a series but independent of it, transcending numerical and temporal infinity. He would no more be first cause *in* the series than a circle is the beginning of its centre.

Even an infinite series of finite causes is not self-explanatory, and yet an explanation is needed. The explanation can only be a being that is not finite; that is, an infinite being. God is known to be infinite because He cannot be finite. A being whose existence is self-explanatory is one to which existence belongs not merely *de facto*, but absolutely and of right: its essence is absolutely identical with existence. No finite being could ever answer to this description, for the essence of any finite being can be conceived adequately as non-existent. A self-explanatory being is totally defined by existence. In it existence has, as it were, absorbed essence as a factor knowable and definable apart from existence.

As has been pointed out already, it is useless to urge that infinite being, too, can be conceived as non-existent. We cannot conceive infinite being directly at all, but can only define it indirectly and judge that it must exist and must be existence unlimited by essence. Useless, again, to urge that a self-explanatory being could be a finite being to which existence belonged of necessity; for the nature of such a being could be conceived clearly and adequately as non-existent. A finite necessary being is a contradiction in terms.

8. *The notion of 'necessary being'*

This would seem to be a convenient place to examine the notion of 'necessary being', about which so much unnecessary fuss has been made in recent years.

From the time of the publication of Kant's *Critique of Pure Reason* until very recently, there was fairly general agreement among non-Catholic philosophers that the Cosmological Argument for the existence of God contained the fallacy of the Ontological Argument. After a hundred and eighty years the tables are gradually turning, and one or two non-scholastic philosophers have come to admit that on this particular point Kant blundered and made a mistake of elementary logic.[1]

However, scholastic philosophers are not to be allowed any respite. Simultaneously with the discarding of one error we are faced with the rise of another. It is now being confidently asserted that St Thomas and his followers made a

[1] cf. J. J. C. Smart, 'The Existence of God' in *New Essays in Philosophical Theology* (ed. Flew and MacIntyre), pp. 36–37.

mistake of elementary logic which would have had a run not of a hundred and eighty years, but of some seven hundred. The Ontological Argument, it is now being said, lurks not exactly where Kant thought it did, but just a little earlier—in fact, as soon as the argument mentions a 'necessary being'.

By a 'necessary being' St Thomas and his followers understand a being whose nature is such that it cannot be non-existent. The objection now being raised on many sides is that a 'necessary being' is a nonsense notion, a contradiction in terms. More fully, an absolutely necessary being means a being whose non-existence is logically impossible: but this is the error of the Ontological Argument which claims that God cannot be thought of as non-existent.[1]

On one important point the objectors are quite right: there are not and there cannot be any logically necessary existential propositions. But what they have overlooked is that St Thomas would agree with them entirely; and he would point out that his argument from the contingence of the world does *not* conclude to the existence of a being whose existence is 'necessary' in the sense of the Ontological Argument.

Let us examine the point in St Thomas's context. In the *Summa Theologica*, 1:2:1, St Thomas refutes the Ontological Argument. In the Third Article of the same Question he propounds the Third Way. On the face of it, it is not very likely that he should so contradict himself at the interval of two or three pages as to deny in one Article what he admits in the next but one—to deny, when refuting the Ontological Argument, that 'God exists' is a logically necessary

[1] Few readers will be inclined to make the mistake of thinking that an 'absolutely necessary being' means one which it is 'absolutely necessary', in the logical sense, to posit as the conclusion of an argument beginning from the existence of the world; though Kant did write in a moment of perversity, 'This supreme cause is then held to be absolutely necessary because it is absolutely necessary to ascend to it.'

proposition, and then to admit it implicitly in the Third Way. The explanation is simple: by a 'necessary being' St Thomas does not mean a 'logically necessary' being; he means a being whose *nature* is such that it could not be non-existent; and such a being is not a logically necessary being. Invited to explain, St Thomas would direct his readers both backward and forward in the *Summa*. He would point out that the refutation of the Ontological Argument means that there are not, and cannot be, any logically necessary existential propositions, not even the proposition 'God exists'. The uniqueness of the proposition 'God exists' makes no essential difference to the point under discussion. What does make the essential difference is the principle announced immediately afterwards in the same Article: '*Nos non scimus de Deo quid est*'—'We do not know what the nature of God is'; which, as has been already pointed out, is a technical use of language meaning that we have of God no direct knowledge, but only indirect, analogical knowledge. Next St Thomas would direct his readers forward, this time to his treatment of our knowledge of God in the thirteenth Question of the First Part. What he there says may be applied to the matter in hand as follows: the cosmological argument concludes to the existence of a being whose *nature* is such that it cannot be non-existent. But since we cannot get this nature of God as it is in itself directly into our minds, 'God exists' cannot be *for us* a logically necessary existential proposition. The matter depends, then, on his doctrine of analogical knowledge of God, a doctrine which to many recent critics of St Thomas seems to be quite unknown.

9. *Efficient causality and the principle of Causality*

It is now time to say something about efficient causality, and the principle of causality, on which the whole argument depends.

Spontaneously, by observation and reflection, most people have always thought that there are efficient causes at work in the world, and that there are effects which really depend, for being what they are, on the cause or causes which produced them; and spontaneously people go on to reflect that if the existence of something is not self-explanatory, there must always be a cause of some kind on which the thing depends for existence, and for being the kind of thing it is. This general formulation is called the principle of causality.

If philosophers come to the conclusion that there is no such thing as real dependence of effect on cause in the world, and that the principle of causality is not objective, they must produce solid reasons; for the evidence that there is real causal dependence in the world, and that the principle of causality applies to the actual world and to all possible reality, seems to be good. In practice we cannot rid ourselves of the notion, in our language, in our thought, in our way of acting. We cannot get far without saying 'because', and it is thought to be a mark of education to be able to distinguish the real cause from attendant circumstances which may seem to be causes but are not. Nothing seems so all-pervasive, so characteristic of the real world as objective cause and effect, effect dependent on cause, cause producing effect. Language is full of the notion. Verbs are active and passive, nouns are subject and object. Most of us earn our living by doing some kind of work. From birth to death, morning to night, in all we do and experience, we take for granted the reality of causal dependence. If the detective is looking for the blunt instrument that broke the man's skull, it seems rather unreal to say that he is looking for the 'antecedent phenomenon', and that nothing really broke the man's skull at all. Did Bacon write Shakespeare? It seems a little unreal to say that, whoever it was, he was only the antecedent phenomenon, and that the plays of Shakespeare do not really owe their existence to any man, any mind, any hand, any pen; that the child does not depend on the parents, nor the disease on the microbe or virus, nor the cure on the penicillin, nor the devastation of Hiroshima on the atom-bomb, nor anything on anything.

It seems necessary to insist a little on these rather obvious matters, because it is the business of philosophy to 'save the appearances'—to provide theories which explain the appearances, so far as possible without remainder.

However, the common sense view of a thing, even if universal and deeply ingrained, is not necessarily the right view, although after due reflection it can be enough for a man's practical needs including his need of finding God. In practice these points, the field of speculation for the philosopher as such, can be seen in the wider context of human life in general, which any normally intelligent person, however innocent of philosophy as a technical subject, may have the power to assess. A man can be reasonably certain of what he can neither express nor prove nor defend; whereas in philosophy one of the rules of the game is that your reasons are worth what they are worth on paper. Still, philosophy is in itself a necessary and good thing, though it would be easily allowed that no philosophy has ever succeeded in expressing or explaining any phenomenon whatever quite adequately; and that sometimes philosophy does more harm than good to people's minds.

The scholastic view of efficient causality is as follows: An efficient cause is that which by its physical influence 'gives' actuality, existence, being of some kind, to another thing. This 'giving' of being is of a unique kind and needs the inverted commas, because it is giving in only an analogical sense. Nothing passes over physically from agent to patient; the agent does not become any the poorer or any the less for causing. The patient acquires something it did not have before, and to that extent is the richer, though the indirect effect may be loss for the patient, as when a man is shot through the heart. Because of the uniqueness of the giving, a uniqueness that makes 'giving' a misleading word, it is admitted that efficient causality is, on the face of it, a mysterious thing; and that while there is enough evidence to be certain that it involves dependence-for-existence, the intimate nature of the dependence is not available to our immediate insight. Another complication is that in some cases there is evident dependence for starting to exist, as in the production of a sheep, but not real dependence on the same causes for continuing to exist. Such is the situation to be analysed, and it is claimed that patient analysis can solve the initial mystery of causality by finding that ultimately all new being is to be attributed to God as well as to finite causes; but this is to leave an inevitable residue of mystery in so far as the causality of God in the world, a causality which in Him is identical with his creative activity and with His essence, is something whose positive possibility we cannot see directly, something we can only conclude to indirectly, though it does not involve any open contradiction.

This dependence of effect on cause is most readily available in our experience of our inner states of mind and will, and next, in the changes we can make in the external world. We can be sure that there is the same dependence of effect on cause in external things among themselves, but there it is often very difficult to isolate the cause or causes of a particular effect. But it is claimed, much further, that the mind can formulate the principle of causality, and recognize it as universally and objectively true not merely in the sphere of experience but in every possible sphere of being: that if a thing starts to exist, or is by some other indication not self-explanatory, then it is dependent on a cause distinct from the effect. To many non-scholastic philosophers this seems a very big claim indeed; but even Kant admitted that we cannot help thinking of it that way. For Kant the explanation of causality was that it is a subjective category of the mind by which we impose a pattern of causality on to experience. For the scholastic philosopher the explanation of the necessity of causality that we feel is that the mind is spiritual, and though not intuitive of individual existents, has the power of understanding not merely this or that individual item of existence and experience, but of generalizing and understanding being as such—the basic requirements and behaviour of all that exists or can exist, not merely because it is *this* piece of existence, this piece of material existence, or even this piece of finite existence, but simply because it *is* something that exists or can exist. It is claimed that one of the things the mind can know about being as such is that if some existence is on any title not self-explanatory, it is to be explained by a cause distinct from the thing to be explained; that finite being as such requires an infinite cause; and that any analysis of experience that would eliminate efficient causes or try to shake the principle of causality, would be a totally inadequate one.

One of the complications is the diversity of types of causes and effects; but this is an advantage in so far as it leads the mind up gradually to understand the nature of cause and effect in general. In material things the agent can produce a new accidental change, a non-essential difference, as when water is poured into a bowl and takes the shape of the bowl. An agent can produce a substantial change, as when food is assimilated and changed into the substance of a human being. In the non-material sphere, a spiritual substance, a human soul, can produce in itself a spiritual accidental change, as when a man thinks or uses his will. New spiritual substances can be produced, as when a new spiritual soul arises in a new human being. This last is considered by Thomists to be a direct creation by God and not a mere natural result of the disposition of the material concerned, in the sense in which other substantial changes are natural results. The soul would thus be pro- duced by God 'out of nothing', and not, in Aristotelean terminology, 'educed from the potency of the matter'. This, while true, might seem to be rather a clumsy and perhaps misleading way of describing something that comes about in the ordinary course of nature. The potentialities of matter are not adequate to the production of spirit; but then, the potentialities of matter are not *adequate* to the production of any change whatever: it can be shown by analysis that any change whatever requires the direct causality of God. Finally, the whole universe with all the causes and effects it contains depends, it is claimed, directly on God for its beginning to be—so far as it does begin to be —and for its continuing to be, and for every real change that takes place within it.

Another division of causes is into *immanent* and *transient.* An immanent cause produces its effect in the same subject, as when a man thinks or a tree grows leaves. A transient effect is produced in another subject, as when a man writes or cuts down a tree.

I now take these different examples and try to analyse them, seeking clues for the understanding of efficient causality as such, so as to be able to analyse the principle of causality and show its objectivity and universality.

To start with the simplest example, what is happening when water is poured into a bowl and takes the shape of the bowl? We say the bowl gives its shape to the water and not *vice versa*. This is really only a way of saying that given water and a hard bowl and the fact that water can be poured in, the water cannot do anything else except take the shape of the bowl: it would be a contradiction for it to do anything else in normal circumstances. It is assumed that things like earthenware and water have natures, and that these can be known to a certain extent. This some philosophers will not allow, although to disallow it is to be unable to explain the induction without which life, science, speech and thought would be impossible. Scholastic philosophers hold that a *nature* is something a thing has, or rather is, simply because it is a thing; something that belongs to all possible being; something without which nothing could exist or be intelligible. That a thing must have a *nature* changeable, but sufficiently stable to be grasped in thought, is a basic principle of being and of knowledge. What the nature of a particular thing is can only be known imperfectly because our minds are not intuitive; but we can know natures in a sketchy way and fill out more or less by induction. But stability of nature and of what is meant by existing nature is basic. This reveals a diametrically opposite attitude to that of empiricism, not merely on the question of what is essence or nature, but also on the question of what is existing nature, as will be seen more in detail when the principle of causality is examined.

In the example under consideration, the nature of the earthenware is to have a certain kind of hardness and resistance to pressure. Water, too, has its own kind of resistance to pressure, but it is not the same as that of the bowl.

When water is poured into a bowl, water and bowl are trying to be in the same place at the same time: the bowl asserts itself in its way and the water asserts itself in its way. The natures of the two being what they are, and the other forces concerned being what they are, nothing else could happen except that the water should yield to the bowl and take its shape. In finite causality, one thing comes within the sphere of influence of another and feels the effect. However unique the giving involved, it seems so far from this example that it is simply something that is bound to happen, given the natures of things and the fact that change is possible. A new reality arises and the effect becomes like the cause because the two things involved are what they are. However, not all examples are as easy as that one, though every kind of example has something special to offer.

Proceeding one step further, what is happening when water turns to ice, or hydrogen and oxygen into water? To take the example of water freezing, water falls in temperature because the lower temperature of the surrounding air allows it to give off its own heat. If the lowering goes far enough it becomes incompatible with the existing behaviour of the molecules of water, and a different behaviour is set up, producing the hard substance called ice. There is some similarity here with water poured into a bowl. In the one case water tends to give off heat, in the other case the water tends to fall, and the surroundings allow it to do so up to a point. When that point is reached, the water conforms itself to the shape, or the temperature, of the surroundings. But in the example of freezing a striking new condition arises, namely hardness. It is a considerable new reality; it could save a man's life or kill him. But it is difficult to say where it comes from. Not directly from the surroundings; they need not have had any hardness to give. The different possible chemical arrangements and behaviours of things are part of the things' natures. We can cause one type of behaviour to be substituted for another, but the possible types of behaviour are just given. This suggests that in such cases it would be misleading to say that the patient is merely passive: it is passive in that it has various types of behaviour and that these can be changed indirectly by various types of external agents; but the types of behaviour are part of the patient's nature; they are present in it virtually rather than merely passively. It is rather like making a car change gear. We can make a car change gear, but we have to accept the gears as we find them; they are part of the possible behaviour of the car.

When a plant grows, chemical substances from outside become part of the plant. In so far as they are recognizable in the plant, their behaviour, considered in isolation, is exactly the same as their behaviour when separate from the plant; though in organic things the elements combine to form molecules of far greater complexity than those of non-living things. But in the living plant the behaviour of the chemical constituents is now subordinated to a new pattern of behaviour which is governed by the nature of the plant—oak, rose or dandelion; just as the behaviour of an alarm-clock is the behaviour of pieces of metal, but subordinated to the behaviour-pattern of an alarm-clock. This new over-all pattern the scholastic philosopher attributes to the nature of the thing, plant, animal or man, calling the nature the *form* as distinct from the matter that is informed. The form of a thing is what the thing essentially *is*, that which gives the thing its characteristic behaviour as the sort of thing it is. This form does not in any way contradict the nature and behaviour of the thing considered as a collection of chemical substances; but it subordinates them to a higher unity which merely as chemical substances they do not have, but which they are capable of serving, as in the example of the alarm-clock.

When a plant, animal or man grows, the process may be looked on from different points of view: it may be seen as one and the same form or idea gradually unfolding its potentialities; or it may be considered as a process of assimilating and organizing new material. If an alarm-clock could be produced which could grow by taking in new material from outside, forming it into new alloys for wheels, tempering it for springs, adding it to wheels to make them grow regularly and differentiate themselves into greater complexity of parts, regulating itself, cleaning itself, winding itself and reproducing itself, and working thus for a number of years, this would be rather like the behaviour of an animal or a tree. Material is capable of being transformed into a tree in that way; the tree is capable of doing it; the material is dealt with in such a way that it is unable to remain mere moisture, but becomes eventually wood, and oak-wood.

In the human body the scholastic theory is that the form is the soul, a spiritual substance capable of separate survival. The soul, in conjunction with the potential element, matter, produces human body which, in its chemical aspects, acts and works in exactly the same way as the same chemical elements would when separated from the body, though they are now organized into highly complex molecules which are associated with living things only. Besides the function of informing the body so as to make it a living body, the soul has the function of thinking. Thought is accidental or non-essential modification of spiritual substance, having corresponding material and physical concomitants such as electricity, and psychological adjuncts such as feeling and imagination, which provide the reminder-images or 'phantasms', as they are called, by reference to which we understand material things, though the conceptual part of our thinking is immaterial. The activity and passivity of a man in growing is like that of a tree. Thought, too, involves activity and passivity in the intellect. When it comes to describing the activity of the mind a special difficulty arises: this cannot be done except in analogical terms, in terms properly applicable to the material sphere only, and applied by transference, and with the necessary adjustment, to the immaterial. This does not mean that nothing simply true can be said about the mind or soul, but it does mean that, whether the terms we use have a specifically material connotation or not, we understand by means of a material, imaginative clue; and when the intelligible content thus grasped is applied to the immaterial, we have to discount the specifically material connotation of the terms used. This process of transference, of understanding the material directly and the immaterial indirectly, is valid and justified, because material and immaterial are both being, and all being has the same essential basic structure and behaviour simply because it is being.

When the material presentation is received by the senses, the mind in its active capacity has the power of penetrating it like a sort of X-ray in such a way as to reveal its intelligible structure. To this the mind responds in its passive capacity, taking the configuration of what the active intellect has revealed. In judging, the mind, or rather the man, is active again, identifying himself with what he finds, making it his own by saying it is true. In this way the intelligibility revealed becomes a more or less permanent part of the man. The concept is less than the individual thing from which it was obtained in so far as it is abstract and does not include the whole intelligibility of the individual; but it is more than the individual in so far as it is purely immaterial and not limited to an individual. By this immaterializing of the thing's intelligibility, the mind is able to understand something not only of this particular individual—triangle, oak-tree, man—but also something about triangle, oak-tree, man in general, about every possible triangle, oak-tree, man: not everything about them, because our minds are not intuitive, but enough about them to distinguish them from other things, and to know things about them that are applicable to every possible specimen of them.

Such in outline is the causality, the activity and passivity, which is involved in thinking. In all thinking there is some engagement of the will, even if only some more or less voluntary attention; but in judging, the will is involved in a special way. By saying something is true, by accepting it, affirming it, we make it our own. There is further activity of the will when we assimilate something not only by saying it is true but by saying it is good, and *my* good. This last is what is done by the free will in moral choice.

In all types of causality, what is common is that the patient comes within the sphere of activity of the agent and feels the effect—an effect which depends both on what the agent is and what the patient is; which produces in the patient a reality which was not there before; a reality which is like the agent in so far as activity is an attempt at union among things, whereby the weaker conforms to the stronger and takes its pattern.

The most striking thing about causality is the one we take most for granted— a thing, too, which is acknowledged even by those who say causality is not objective: the fact that these changes involve new reality, new intelligibility, new goodness, new values, new being. It is not that there is mere

substitution or change of position, though even that would
pose a problem, but that very often there is new development, new excellence. In a true sense, where there was
nothing there is now something. All genius and its work,
Homer and Virgil, Dante and Shakespeare, Newton and
Einstein: they were not, and then they were; and there was
produced each one's *monumentum aere perennius*. Where has it
come from? From its causes, yes. But the causes, whatever
they were, lose nothing, sacrifice nothing, in giving. From
the minds themselves in so far as they were enriched by
outside causes, and developed themselves, yes. But however
much active and passive potentiality is admitted, and however true it is that finite causes are true causes, the mystery
remains: where has the new being come from? Because it
seems to have come from nothing, from the nothingness of
itself. Potentiality is only our word for the fact that, in the
normal course of things and in certain definite and regular
ways, things can develop and enrich one another, and new
being can arise; and not merely new arrangements of old
things, as the chemist may see it from one point of view,
but new and greatly enhanced intelligibility; that is, new
and greatly enhanced being. Now I say this is a great problem and a great mystery. The new being was never in the
agents; it was not in the patient; and then it was in the
patient. If those were the only factors involved, there would
be an insoluble problem, and it would be impossible to give
a reasonable answer to Parmenides when he claimed that
change is an impossibility. This to my mind points immediately to the fact that the only way to make reasonable sense
of any real change whatever is to postulate an infinite cause
in all finite causality. Only an infinite cause can produce
new being without contradiction: for the finite adds nothing
univocal to the infinite. We have no direct insight into how

the infinite *can* cause the finite: it is reasonably intelligible in that it does not involve open contradiction; but to try to explain causality without an infinite agent *does* involve open contradiction if the principle of causality, that nothing can come from nothing, is true.

The principle of causality. First I will describe the principle of causality as a claim, and see to what extent it is supported by common sense. This will provide the situation to be justified philosophically. The principle of causality is founded on the claim that it is possible and necessary to ask the question, Why do things exist? and that the answer, about any particular thing or type of thing must be *either* that the thing exists simply and absolutely in its own right, that it completely explains its own existence, and that it is not possible or necessary to look further for an explanation of its existence; *or* that the thing does not explain its own existence, that it depends for its existence on an efficient cause. The claim is that God alone belongs to the first category, and all finite being belongs to the second.

If a thing is observed to come into existence, people say spontaneously that it must have a cause, that nothing can start to exist without a cause. This is the most obvious example of what is spontaneously thought of as a case for causal dependence, and it is based on the common-sense principle which, the Thomist claims, is also a necessary metaphysical principle, that 'nothing can come from nothing'.

But at this point common sense encounters something of a puzzle. Granted that a thing which begins to be must have a cause, is it clear that it requires a cause of continuing to be? In some cases this is evidently so: water which takes the shape of the bowl needs the same cause in order to continue to be that shape; ice needs a low temperature to continue to

be ice. But on the other hand, a sheep needs parent sheep
for its beginning to exist, but not for continuing to exist. It
is true that once in existence a sheep needs many things in
order to continue to be a sheep, air, food, heat, and so on;
but at the same time, by simply being a sheep it has something which of its very nature tends to exist, an intrinsic
dynamism which asserts and maintains itself, which is, in
fact, what it means to exist. It seems at first sight that such
a dynamism would itself be an excellent and sufficient
reason why a sheep or anything else should go on existing.
Many things need many other things in order to remain the
sort of things they are. But whatever happens, and however
much things may have to yield to *force majeure*, still, *force
majeure* is always available, and prevails and maintains itself
in one place or another, and the world as a whole obstinately
clings to existence; and, in fact, is evolving, in some parts at
any rate, towards greatly enhanced perfection: though
whether the universe as a whole is conserving or dissipating
its energy is another matter.

If the principle of causality claims that a finite thing
which has the dynamism of existence needs a cause which is
maintaining precisely this dynamism, here is something
which goes beyond everyday common sense. Common sense
here recognizes a puzzle for which philosophers may be able
to give an answer. The Thomist claims that every existing
finite thing whatever, material or spiritual, is such a dynamism which is being maintained in that condition by God,
without whose causality it would relapse into nothingness.

Historically, most philosophers have agreed with common sense upon that section of the matter of causality which
is most readily available to our understanding, viz., that if a
thing begins to be it must have an efficient cause. It is only
comparatively recently that there has been a thorough-

going philosophical attack on the objectivity of causality, the two chief attackers in their different ways being Hume and Kant. Similarly scientists have until much more recently always accepted causality in their own field, at least as something applicable to phenomena or as a working hypothesis that has yielded excellent results. Some scientists question it nowadays in one restricted field, though even here they admit it is applicable to the aggregate, though not to each separate item. Other scientists question or deny the exclusion of causality even from this limited field for various reasons scientific or philosophical, e.g. because the scientific definition of the particles involved is too vague to be a sound basis for the conclusions drawn about them.[1] Thus it has not yet become evident, even on the principles of a science that would like to feel emancipated from metaphysics, that the spirited attack on Epicurus in Cicero's *De Finibus* (I, vi) no longer stands: 'He says the atom moves out of the straight line without a cause: now surely, to say that anything happens without a cause is the last thing one would expect from a respectable physical philosopher.'

Hume argued that because we can know that first a thing did not exist and then it began to exist, and because we can think of these two states without joining them by the notion of cause, therefore there is no rational justification for postulating a cause.[2] It is true that we can abstract from the notion of cause in that way, and consider simply before and

[1] cf. Professor G. Temple, F.R.S., 'Physics and Philosophy,' in *Catholic Approaches* (ed. Lady Pakenham).

[2] I am aware that Hume wrote: 'I never asserted so absurd a Proposition as *that any thing might arise without a Cause*' (Letter to John Stewart, 1754). But that statement, in the context of his philosophy, means that the principle of causality, in so far as it is considered to be objective, is a matter only of inescapable belief which must be accepted in ordinary life; but that the principle is neither self-evident nor demonstrable nor otherwise intelligible to us.

after, like two pictures placed side by side; but the question is, would that be an *adequate* analysis? In the old story a twist of the ring made the wearer invisible. Could it be possible for a thing—this book, say, or, for that matter, the whole universe—not merely to alternate between being visible and invisible, but between existence and absolute extinction, *without any cause or reason whatever*? According to extreme empiricism it would be possible. According to common sense and most philosophers before Hume, it would not. The empiricist view amounts to saying that the whole universe could come into being from absolutely nothing, with no cause or reason at all. Lear answers in the name of sanity: 'Nothing will come of nothing: speak again.' People differ. To some, the empiricist analysis seems merely a refreshing example of what happens when one rids oneself of a stubborn prejudice, something on a par with realizing that after all the sun does not go round the earth. To others, such an analysis of causality, presented as adequate, seems a monstrosity and an affront to human reason. Hume attributes the mind's expectance of a cause merely to habit and association; we have never seen it otherwise, so we feel it cannot be otherwise. But to begin with, the fact that we have never seen it otherwise is part of the phenomenon to be explained. And further, to say that the items of our experience which we call causes are not causes at all and that there is no real causal dependence in the world, seems to most minds to make nonsense of life and speech and thought. Kant's explanation has at least a *prima facie* plausibility; the contention that no explanation is needed has none. If common sense is right about causality, then the empiricist picture-philosophy must be completely out of touch with reality; and so I think it is.

Kant admits that we feel the necessity of a cause, but

attributes this feeling to a subjective category of the mind, which imposes the notion of causality on the sense-appearances. Thus the judgment that a new event must have a cause is called by him 'synthetic *a priori*'; synthetic, because 'new event' does not contain the idea of 'cause'; *a priori* because the necessity of joining the two notions is felt independently of experience and is attributed to every possible experience. And why not? it may be asked. Does not Kant's proposal very neatly account for the necessity of principles like that of causality—a necessity that goes beyond experience? Kant's theory would to that extent be plausible if the necessity could not be accounted for in any other way. But the scholastic philosopher is able to account for it in another way. He claims that the immaterial mind has the power to generalize, so as to understand the notion of being-as-such, as that which exists or can exist, and all the most general principles contained in or derived from that notion. One of these principles is that of causality. The principle that a thing which begins to be, or is otherwise not self-explanatory, must have an efficient cause, must be involved in the notion of being. To deny the principle of causality must be to deny being in one of its aspects: it must be implicitly a contradiction in terms, when the terms are existential.

Moreover, Kant's revolutionary philosophy, though plausible in some of its general lines, is not so when applied in detail. It is not plausible, after all Kant's explanations, to say that our experience of sea and sky and oak-trees and our friends and family and pens and paper-clips leaves the nature and very existence of things in themselves wholly problematic. Again, Kant proposes his theory of the subjective nature of space and time, and of the categories of the understanding like that of causality, because of the contradictions which, he alleges, are brought to light if one considers these conditions as objective. With regard to 'finding the unconditioned', i.e. God, as the efficient cause of the conditioned things of our experience, he says that the deceptive character of this illusion (that causality is objective) would not be observed if it did not betray itself by the self-contradiction into which reason falls when it seeks to apply the principle that the conditioned presupposes the unconditioned. But all the contradictions alleged by Kant, in the spheres of both sensibility and understanding, are of his own manufacture. In the present instance he points out that one can always, and must always, suppose a cause of every phenomenon of experience, and a cause of that cause, and so on *ad infinitum*; but that to suppose an unconditioned cause would be to interrupt this necessarily infinite series: therefore our conception of cause, if treated as objective, leads to a contradiction. This is pure imagination on Kant's part. There is no contradiction in thinking that a series of finite causes should be started and terminated and caused in its entirety by the unconditioned cause, God; and if an infinite series is a possibility, there is no difficulty in supposing that it is in its entirety caused by God. God is not at one end of the series, but transcends it. As for the difficulty that God, too, must be thought of as having a cause, this is to be betrayed not by the constitution of the human mind, but once more by the imagination. To know what God is, is to know that He is not and cannot be caused; it is to see that the cause which must be postulated for finite things cannot apply to Him.

It is significant to say that the universe we know exists. If it is required to put the fact of existence into terms of subject and predicate, one may say if one pleases that existence is a predicate but a different sort of predicate.

Existence is not an essence like triangle, tree, or man, yet it has a significance which is grasped through experience and affirmed in the judgment of existence. It is what makes the difference between a thing as possible and as actual. We do not think of everything as existing, as some contemporaries allege; we think of everything as either existing or as able to exist. It is this existence that we are now trying to appreciate.

Existing things are what we can come up against, and what can come up against us. They are not merely things we have thought up for ourselves; though even imaginary things exist as modifications of our minds. Existing things present themselves as assertions, thrusts into the universe, and not at all like mere pictures flickering on a screen. From a tin-tack to an atom-bomb they assert themselves vigorously, and we ignore them at our peril. Hume's assertion that experience gives us events following one another, but never any idea of 'force or power' by which a cause operates, is just about as wrong as it could be. The idea of 'force or power' is absolutely inseparable from that of existing being; it is part of its very meaning. It is even inseparable from something considered in the state of mere possibility; for even the essence of a thing is inconceivable except as something that acts on my mind, as something I must submit to if I want to know it. As for Kant, his whole philosophy, like everyone else's, is a statement of the reason why things appear to us as they do; and the reason why, found in existing things, is precisely the cause.

Hume allows that existence and non-existence are contraries. I suggest that to say that finite being comes to exist, or exists, without a cause involves a contradiction; so that Hume would be equivalently saying that existence is non-existence. I do not mean that Hume would be saying that *this* piece of existence is *this* piece of non-existence; I mean that Hume is contradicting the nature of existence by saying that existence can do what it cannot do, or that non-existence can do what only existence can do. It is only by reducing existence to a picture that Hume is able to make his theory for a moment plausible. As he himself says, consistently enough with his theory of knowledge, the separation of the idea of cause from that of a beginning is 'plainly possible for the *imagination*', as though the pictorial image of a thing were the whole account of it. Existence, it is here claimed against Hume, cannot be understood except as dynamism; and to say that dynamism can start or stop without reason is to have failed to face what it means. What ought rather to cause surprise is that *anything* can cause existence in any form to start or stop; to say *nothing* is needed to cause it to start or stop is to contradict its very nature. To reflect on this is to find the reason for the shock which the mind cannot but experience at the suggestion that anything can begin to be without a cause.

Human knowledge is a mixture of abstraction and intuition; but, however one explains it, and wherever in human knowledge one places the core of this matter, it is certain that every act of knowledge immediately and inescapably recognizes existence as dynamism. The apprehension of it is rather like the pressure of the moral conscience, which is, in fact, only a particular case of the dynamism of existence. Existence is presented peremptorily. It cannot be permanently ignored: *usque recurret*. And it insists that being, that which exists or can exist, can only be understood as dynamism; that finite existence, as finite dynamism, is changeable, indeed, but of its nature, and in its measure, enduring; and if it arises, it arises from existence; and its arising, far from being no mystery at all, is a great mystery, and one that begins to make sense only if we postulate an infinite source of all finite existence, God.

10. *Kant's objections to the Cosmological and Teleological Arguments*

It is still widely held that Kant's criticism of the Cosmological and Teleological ('physico-theological') Arguments has disposed of them once for all. On the other hand we find the view that 'seldom has a philosopher presented so uncritical and sophistical a critique as that presented here by the sage of Königsberg'.[1]

Kant gives the Cosmological Argument in a very brief but acceptable form from Leibniz: If anything exists, an absolutely necessary being exists; now, at least I myself exist; *ergo* . . . He allows that the argument starts from experience. He allows further that we may conclude from it that some sort of necessary being exists. But he claims that to pass from the conception of a necessary being to that of 'being of the highest reality' is the same process as that of the Ontological Argument. Kant does not allow that 'necessary being' is simply identical with infinite being: for him, necessary being could be the world of our experience. His objection therefore is equivalently that the only meaning of 'necessary being' which is of any use to the Cosmological Argument is one which *is* identical with infinite being. But such a concept, on Kant's principles, has lost touch with existence, has entered the 'transcendental' region of mere conceptions, and needs to regain contact with existence by means of the Ontological Argument. Thus the real point of the objection is that the Cosmological Argument is inconclusive *granted Kant's theory of knowledge:* but it does not

[1] cf. B. Jansen, *La philosophie religieuse de Kant (Die Religionsphilosophie Kants*, translated and adapted by Pierre Chaillet), p. 70.

follow that it is inconclusive for those who do not accept Kant's theory of knowledge; and it is certainly not so on St Thomas's theory of knowledge.

For Kant, as has been said, the category of causality applies only to experience, and even within experience it is merely a subjective frame for unifying phenomena. When applied beyond experience, and so when applied to God's alleged causality, it cannot have even this limited subjective function. It is true that for Kant the formal structure of knowledge, culminating in the idea of God, provides the mind with an ideal of unity towards which it ever strives to approach in the understanding of experience; but this unity is purely ideal, in Kant's phrase 'regulative, not constitutive'; and nothing objective corresponds to any idea which takes us beyond experience, though he admits that the mind is irresistibly impelled to seek ever greater unity of understanding within this subjective framework. For the Thomist, on the other hand, the principle of causality has objective reference not only within experience but beyond it. The irresistible impulse of the mind which Kant admits is an objective insight into the structure of being; and the conclusion to the ultimate and original cause of all contingent being is valid and objective, however true it is that it presents us with a cause and a type of causality only analogically similar to the causes of our experience. The necessary being to which St Thomas and his followers conclude is therefore existent being, and not a mere notion. The argument has left experience, but it has not left existent reality; and there is therefore no need to invoke the Ontological Argument in order to regain contact with existence.

In his summary at the end of his main objections, Kant mentions another alleged 'sophism' of the Cosmological Argument, namely 'the inference to a first cause from the impossibility of an infinite series of causes being presented one after another in the world of sense'. As I have mentioned several times already, the Cosmological Argument does not in the least depend on the impossibility of an infinite series of causes presented either one after another or simultaneously in the world of sense or beyond it. Here again Kant is interpreting in the framework of his own epistemology.

In his objections to the Teleological Argument (called by Kant 'physico-theological'), he proceeds as follows. He concentrates on the adaptation of many different things in the world to a single end, i.e. he concentrates on external finality; and argues that even if it be granted that there is such finality, we should not be justified in concluding that it is due to a *creator*, but only to an *architect* of the universe; that the argument proves contingence merely in the form of the world, and not in its 'matter or substance'; that the architect of the universe would be very much limited by the adaptability of the material in which he works; and that to establish the contingence of the matter, the argument would need to have recourse to the Cosmological Argument, with all its 'transcendental illusions'.

To pause at this point we may reply first that it is better to consider *internal* finality, the order or intelligibility of individual things, than external finality. Next, to Kant's distinction between creator and architect it must be said that the argument he criticizes is essentially one from intelligibility to intellect; and as such, bears not merely on the pattern of external finality, and not merely on the form or internal order of material things, but also on their very matter itself. Matter in the scientist's sense is very highly ordered and intelligible; while matter in the Aristotelean and Thomist sense, pure potentiality for the reception of forms, is by itself nothing actual or intelligible, yet in combination with form it constitutes a material thing which is intelligible as a whole, and in which even the matter is indirectly intelligible in its relation to form. Thus the whole of a material thing exhibits intelligibility, in spite of the fact that from another point of view matter is a principle of limitation of form and intelligibility. When seen in this radical sense, the intelligibility of the material world exhibits the total dependence which points to a creator, not a mere architect. And creation, total dependence, does not begin to be moderately intelligible except on the supposition of an infinite cause which can produce finite being without producing more being.

Kant then proceeds to urge the same objection from a different point of view. The argument, he says, seeks to find a cause adequate to the production of the order of the world: on the other hand, the only cause which is of any use as the conclusion of the argument would be an infinite cause, God. 'Now, I do not think anyone will be bold enough to claim he can see how the greatness of the world as he has observed it is related, in content or extent, to omnipotence; how the order of the world is related to supreme wisdom, or the unity of the world to the absolute unity of its author.' As has been pointed out, if the argument from intelligibility did no more than show an intellect, it would be a great point gained. But, in fact, it does more than this; for intelligibility is in the last analysis identical with being; and contingent intelligibility requires a ground of infinite intelligibility, just as contingent being requires a ground of infinite being. 'Thus the physico-theological proof, baffled in its attempt . . . suddenly falls back on the cosmological proof.' There is no question of the one argument falling back on the other; the two arguments are essentially identical.

9

Some Controverted Arguments

1. *The Fourth Way of St Thomas*

THE Fourth Way of St Thomas reads as follows:

> The *Fourth Way* is taken from the degrees (of perfection) which
> are found in things. We find in the world the more and less
> good, more and less true, more and less noble, and so of other
> perfections of that type. But 'more' and 'less' are said to belong
> to different things in so far as they approach in their different
> degrees to something which is 'most'—just as a thing which has
> more heat is nearer to that which has most heat. Therefore there
> is something which is true and good and noble in the highest
> degree, something, that is, which has being in the highest
> degree. . . . But that which is said to have 'most' of a quality
> of some kind, is the cause of all things of that kind, just as fire,
> which has most heat, is the cause of all hot things, as Aristotle
> says. . . . Therefore there exists something which is the cause
> of being and goodness and every kind of perfection in the
> world; and this we call God.

I have already pointed out by implication how in my
opinion this Fourth Way is to be interpreted, and little need
be added here. One may, however, take the opportunity of
saying that unnecessary difficulty has been created by some
interpreters through misunderstanding the stance, so to call
it, of the Five Ways, so that the Fourth Way in particular

has been approached too literally. There is a casualness about the presentation of the Five Ways which seems due to the fact that St Thomas is not writing for readers who have any doubt about the existence of God. He is merely offering avenues of approach, possible analyses in terms of reason, of the certainty which his readers already possessed. It is as though he said, 'You can have sight of the summit by taking this route'; he does not imply that he here intends to act as guide to the reader over every step of the way. There may be ravines to cross about which he says nothing; and I think this is true in the present instance.

As it stands, the Fourth Way looks like what is called the Platonic approach; that is, an approach that takes for granted that there is a reality corresponding to every idea of ours; and—further, perhaps, than we have any distinct warrant for going even in Plato—that we can ascend in this way to see the possibility of infinite being, and that therefore there exists a reality corresponding to it. I suggest that the Fourth Way could be paraphrased as follows:

> We observe in the world degrees of perfection in what are called the transcendentals—being, unity, truth, goodness. These degrees suggest to our mind a maximum—immediately, no doubt, a relative maximum, just as Aristotle thought that fire was the hottest thing ever actually found; but they also suggest an absolute maximum; and we think of finite degrees as 'participating' in this maximum in the Platonic manner, finding the the idea spontaneously attractive, but not feeling certain at first how to justify it. Now, this absolute or infinite maximum is, in fact, what we mean by God; and the finite degrees of being do in fact participate in His being, and do so because He is their efficient cause, just as Aristotle says fire is the efficient cause of lower degrees of heat.

If we ask St Thomas whether we know the real possibility of

this maximum simply by considering the idea, or simply as it is suggested to our minds by degrees of being, he will answer, consistently with his refutation of the Ontological Argument, with his whole treatment of our knowledge of God, and with his whole metaphysic as I understand it, that we do not know the possibility *a priori* nor simply by ascending through degrees of being; but that we know it as the term of a process of thought which begins with the finite of experience, and, in considering it, soon catches up with the spontaneous, though at first problematic, flight of the mind from finite to infinite. For degrees of being are necessarily finite; and as finite they are not self-explanatory, but require an infinite efficient cause; so that the absolute maximum which their degrees of perfection suggest to our minds is indeed found to be justified, to exist, and to be no mere flight of the imagination.

St Thomas, writing at the end of eight hundred years of Augustinian tradition, is much too human, apart from considerations of history and philosophy, to say, 'I don't quite agree with Augustine on this point.' He takes other opportunities of inserting his Aristotelean complement to Plato, notably his treatment of the Ontological Argument.

2. *The argument from moral obligation*

I now pass to a brief consideration of one or two other arguments, proposed by some scholastic philosophers as valid, by others as doubtful, and rejected by others as simply invalid. The first is the argument from moral obligation.

It is sometimes said that if one wants to offer a reason for the existence of God to the ordinary man, the man in the railway carriage, one will probably have most success with the argument from moral obligation. This may be true, but it does not settle the question whether the argument is philosophically valid, though it presents a phenomenon which needs explaining. The argument may be stated as follows: All men in some circumstances acknowledge the fact of moral obligation, namely, that there are some things which they are absolutely obliged in conscience to do or to avoid; that this obligation cannot be explained merely as a standard which I set up for myself and may change and abandon at will; not merely as a standard imposed on me by social pressure; not merely as something imposed by human nature as the fitting or attractive thing to do; not merely as something that depends on foreseeable results to myself or to others; but as something so absolute and in-escapable that it cannot be adequately explained by any cause whatever within our experience; that its adequate cause must lie partly at least outside our experience; that this cause must include a person with absolute authority over human persons; and that such a person can only be God. Among scholastic philosophers opinion is about equally divided between those who accept the argument, those who reject it, and those who hold that it is no more than probable or suasive. St Thomas does not propose it explicitly at all. As it stands, and in isolation, I do not think the argument is more than probable; but the question remains whether by taking any philosophical argument quite in isolation one is not in some important respect put-ting an unnatural strain on human reason.

According to the Aristotelean and Thomist conception, all being is dynamic: not a mere idea, a flitting picture on a screen, but an assertion, a thrust into the world. Existence asserts itself simply by being—by being a particular kind of thing and continuing to be so as long as it can, and, when it no longer can, by changing, if it is material, into some other kind of being. What is, tries to go on being, and, according to its potentialities, to develop itself; but even mere continuance in existence is a kind of development, an expression of dynamism. This is the first basic fact to be considered when analysing moral obligation. Man's dynamism is beyond all comparison more intense than that of matter, because man's soul is essentially immaterial and spiritual. An atom-bomb may blast his body, but it cannot blast his soul. His soul, because it is spirit, cannot be destroyed by any created power at all; it is intrinsically or of its very nature indestructible. And this dynamism of man's soul bears him, in fact, not merely beyond this life but inexorably towards God, his last end. It is against a thrust or dynamism of this intensity that a man tries to pit the strength of his free will when he denies his nature by moral evil. The question is whether the experience of moral evil is of such a quality that it can be explained sufficiently by only a part of this dynamism, that part which is experienced in this world. The dynamism is, of course, towards good, because towards being. The good of man as such is moral good; the evil of man as such is moral evil. Physical evil is only the evil of his body; he can reconcile himself to that even to death. Can he reconcile himself, even to death, with the evil of his soul, of his real self? And if he cannot, does that mean that God has made him so, and made him feel so?

The experience of moral good and evil is, then, the experience of having our free will either in line with or out of line with our human nature. In moral evil the nature thrusts in one direction, the free will in the opposite direction. We say, that is my good, when our nature tells us through our conscience that it is not. A man is conscious of this, at least implicitly; and he is conscious in the same way that as long as he persists in that internal conflict he cannot

be happy—any more than he can be comfortable if, in contradiction of his physical nature, he holds his hand in the
fire. In this state of mind he faces the future. In denying his
nature by moral evil he has put himself also out of harmony
with his fellow men. He knows that they punish some forms
of moral evil by law, other forms by ostracism; and that he
cannot be at one with them so long as he is not at one with
himself. Historically this situation has often made men fear
a future life; but it seems doubtful whether the moral order
by itself would make the average man certain of a future
life, or certain of the existence of God who would make the
whole into an intelligible order of justice. It seems that the
inescapable dynamism of the human spirit is sufficient to
account for the experience of moral obligation. Does the
dynamism necessarily imply God as its explanation? In so
far as it is an example of finite being, it does. What is added
by the special quality of obligation to be in harmony with
one's own finite nature? It is sometimes said that the absoluteness of moral obligation is inexplicable without the
Absolute. But this is no more than to say that the finite is
inexplicable without the infinite. The absoluteness of finite
being is merely an aspect of its being. By moral obligation,
then, a man can have a heightened awareness that the order
in which he finds himself is one which, of its nature, tends to
good. He can be led to suspect that this implies an order of
justice involving a future life; that this in turn implies a
Person who alone can be thought to have authority over all
possible human persons; and that this Person is the goal,
as He is also the source, of the dynamism of all being and
most especially of human persons. Further than that it does
not seem that one can very confidently go.

To return to the ordinary man, the man in the railway
carriage. It may be taken for granted that if he is impressed

by one argument, there will in fact be more at work in his mind than that. If the argument from moral obligation is only doubtfully valid, why is it so impressive? The answer would seem to be that it speaks to a person of a Person; and this is bound to engage an ordinary man's real apprehension far more than an argument in terms of finite and infinite, conditioned and absolute. And if the fact of a Person is not altogether evident from moral obligation simply as such, yet it is evident from moral obligation in another of its aspects, namely, as an example of intelligibility. A man can know spontaneously and with certainty that the ultimate ground and explanation of a person cannot be less than a person; that only an original Intellect can explain the intelligibility of the world; and in moral obligation he is invited to find this Intellect looking into his most intimate and secret self in the one situation in which he can, if he so wills, deny his nature and by doing so deny its Maker.

3. *The argument from desire of happiness*

Another approach to the existence of God sometimes put forward is through the desire of happiness; but it seems that this is not as strong even as the approach through moral obligation. The argument may take the following form: We have an innate, ineradicable desire of happiness; and this desire is never satisfied by any finite good; therefore it can only be explained by the existence of infinite good. It seems that an argument of this kind is sufficiently shaken by the fact that the desire for happiness which people have is in many cases quite insufficient to convince a man even of the fact of immortality, let alone of an infinite object which we can desire to possess. It seems rather that, in many cases at least, the decision to 'lay hold on eternal life' and to live for an eternity possessing and possessed by God, is taken as a duty consequent on conviction through other reasons, or else from belief in revelation, rather than as a response to an innate spontaneous desire. We do desire to know what is true and to possess whatever in general is our good; but this mere desire is no proof that there exists an infinite truth and an infinite good. We can desire efficaciously only what we know to be possible; and the strength or quality of human desire alone is no sufficient warrant of the existence or possibility of infinite truth or goodness. Once it has been shown by some other way that infinite good is possible and exists, we can conclude that we can and ought to desire it; but the mere dynamism of intellect and will does not seem to me to prove directly a corresponding infinite object. Here all that was said in treating the Ontological Argument seems applicable.

What, then, are we to make of St Augustine's best-known saying, 'Thou hast made us for Thyself, O Lord, and our hearts are restless till they rest in Thee'? The words are true, but I think their bearing is rather different from that of the argument just examined. Man is indeed made for God in the sense that his last end is the possession of God in eternal life; that in this life he is meant to find certainty about God's existence, and to love Him and serve Him; and finally to recognize God's revelation of Himself in Christ and to accept it. Such is man's whole *raison d'être*; and if he fulfils it he will find a basic peace and fulfilment of mind and will and heart which he cannot have otherwise. It can, therefore, be said that the disquiet which is present when a man's mind and will have not found their connatural object in this life is a stimulus to go on searching. But it does not seem of itself to indicate what will be the end of the search or even, necessarily, that the search is destined to have any notable result at all. Very many people do not feel the need to assume that because they have natural desires, these desires can or will find a wholly satisfying object. Restlessness of mind and heart might, on the face of it, be an inherent human condition from first to last, and in fact it remains so at some levels, even for men who already know and love God; while to take the line that 'God exists because He satisfies my felt needs' would be a dangerous thing indeed.

On the other hand, the desire of happiness, and the surmise of God's existence to which it may very well give rise are part of the cry of the human heart *ripae ulterioris amore* which God means to satisfy by the light He sheds on the world. This light bids men look both within themselves and without, and there find that God's existence is a reasonable and necessary conclusion, though it is a conclusion that will seldom if ever be simply a matter of cold reason. Man is more than pure reason, though everything in man must face reason's scrutiny. The light God offers is more than the light of reason, in that reason can see that special revelation is a possibility, and historically a claim offered to his investigation, containing a message which, if it is indeed God's, will not fail to help him towards certainty about the existence of its Author.

4. *The consent of mankind*

The consent of mankind, so far as there is consent, is not without weight when one tries to assess the evidence for God's existence. Ultimately, of course, it is worth exactly what mankind's reasons are worth; but in a matter of this kind and extent it is fair to assume that mankind's reasons are worth something. With all its limitations, it is an impressive phenomenon. But one cannot be blind to its limitations.

The ancient Greeks were one of the most intelligent races the world has ever seen, but they were not remarkably quick to arrive at a genuine, recognizable monotheism. It is true that all the ancient Greek philosophers save the sceptics had a natural theology of some kind; that they all, with the same exception, held one or more ultimate realities and readily gave it or them the name of God or gods. But on the whole they were not quick to see the need of infinite spirit, and it would seem to beg the question to suppose that they were all groping towards this conclusion.

On the other hand, among the very great philosophers of ancient Greece, Plotinus explicitly defended the existence of infinite spirit; and he found this implicit in Plato's Idea of the Good which was 'beyond essence'. Plato himself is full of the idea of divine providence in the world. Aristotle could have concluded to infinite spirit with the principles he hammered out for himself, yet he failed to reach that conclusion. The Stoics had an intellectual first principle of the world which they strangely called 'body' yet contrasted with matter. It was for them the soul of the world, not apart from the world. Yet the Stoics provide some of the finest pages in any literature in praise of divine providence. In earlier days, Xenophanes had protested against the anthropomorphic gods, and called for the recognition of 'One God, the greatest among gods and men, neither in form like unto mortals nor in mind', who 'without toil sways all things with the thought of his mind'. About the same period Parmenides seems to have been not far in thought, however far he was in expression, from the idea of infinite spirit. Melissus, his follower, saw, if we may take the scanty evidence on its face value, that Parmenides's *One* must be both infinite and without body. And again in the pre-Socratic period Heraclitus postulated a Logos or Reason ordering the universe, but it was, it seems, immanent in it and not transcending it.

For the rest, in the Western world the acceptance of God is very largely bound up with revealed religion, Judaism and Christianity. I have tried to assess the significance of this in a previous section.

INDEX

1. NAMES

2. SUBJECTS

211
G67